To World

Juan Gelman (Buenos Aires, 1930–Mexico City, 2014), the most read, influential, and renowned Latin American poet of our times, published more than 30 books of poetry and won countless awards including the Cervantes Prize (2007), the top literary honor in Spanish-language literature. Both a literary and moral paradigm within and outside Argentina, Gelman worked as a journalist and translator, spent many years exiled in Europe and Latin America, and remained an ardent critic of imperialist politics and human rights violations throughout his life. Here, for the first time in English, is his 2008 collection *Mundar/To World*, one of the masterpieces of his later poetry.

To World
Mundar
MEXICO CITY / 2004–2007

JUAN GELMAN

Translated by
KATHERINE M. HEDEEN
and VÍCTOR RODRÍGUEZ NÚÑEZ

CROMER

PUBLISHED BY SALT
12 Norwich Road, Cromer NR27 0AX, United Kingdom

All rights reserved

© The Estate of Juan Gelman 2014
English translations and introduction
© Katherine M. Hedeen and Víctor Rodríguez-Núñez 2014

The right of Juan Gelman to be identified as the
author of this work has been asserted by his estates in accordance
with Section 77 of the Copyright, Designs and Patents Act 1988.

This book is in copyright. Subject to statutory exception
and to provisions of relevant collective licensing agreements,
no reproduction of any part may take place without the written
permission of Salt Publishing.

Salt Publishing 2014

Printed and bound in the United States by Lightning Source Inc.

Typeset in Swift 9.5 / 13

*This book is sold subject to the conditions that it shall not,
by way of trade or otherwise, be lent, re-sold, hired out,
or otherwise circulated without the publisher's prior consent
in any form of binding or cover other than that in which
it is published and without a similar condition including this
condition being imposed on the subsequent purchaser.*

ISBN 978 1 84471 986 0 paperback

1 3 5 7 9 8 6 4 2

Contents

La manzana	2
The Apple	3
Compañeros	4
Comrades	5
El pato salvaje	6
The Wild Duck	7
Amistades	8
Friendships	9
Escondrijos	10
Hideaways	11
La alondra	12
The Lark	13
Debajo	14
Below	15
Ahí	16
There	17
Accidentes	18
Accidents	19
La conversación con Mara esta noche	20
The Conversation with Mara Tonight	21
Líneas	22
Lines	23
Callejones	24
Alleyways	25
Cosmos	26
Cosmos	27
Tarde	28
Evening	29
El niño	30

The Child	31
Lejanías	32
Distances	33
Alas	34
Wings	35
Poema	36
Poem	37
A ver	38
Let's See	39
Roces	40
Brushings	41
La extranjera	42
The Foreigner	43
Vienen cómo	44
How They Come	45
Jardines	46
Gardens	47
Islas	48
Islands	49
La carta	50
The Letter	51
Océanos	52
Oceans	53
Regiros	54
Re-turns	55
Pasados	56
Pasts	57
Qué	58
What	59
Sacar	60
To Draw Out	61

Hilos	62
Threads	63
El barranco	64
The Barranca	65
Saludo	66
Greeting	67
Soneto	68
Sonnet	69
Paco	70
Paco	71
La pregunta	72
The Question	73
Olvidos	74
Oversights	75
Sucederá	76
It Will Happen	77
¿Cómo se llama?	78
What's It Called?	79
Tardes	80
Evenings	81
Sépase	82
Be It Known	83
Albas	84
Dawns	85
Patria	86
Homeland	87
Canción	88
Song	89
¿Cuánto?	90
How Much?	91
En	92

In	93
Andrea escribe a Marcela	94
Andrea Writes to Marcela	95
El encuentro	96
The Encounter	97
Amparos	98
Shelters	99
Avenidas	100
Avenues	101
Pisadas	102
Hoofprints	103
Malena	104
Malena	105
Es	106
Is	107
Tango	108
Tango	109
Foto	110
Photo	111
Andrea	112
Andrea	113
Volver	114
To Return	115
Pedazos	116
Pieces	117
Alrededor	118
Around	119
Baires	120
Baires	121
Gorri	122
Gorri	123

La pretensión	124
The Aspiration	125
El estornino	126
The Starling	127
Lecturas	128
Readings	129
Azares	130
Fates	131
Las águilas	132
The Eagles	133
Piojos	134
Lice	135
Plato	136
Plate	137
La camisa	138
The Shirt	139
Otoñar	140
To Autumn	141
Habilidades	142
Skills	143
La diosa	144
The Goddess	145
Problemas	146
Problems	147
Espasmos	148
Spasms	149
El puñal	150
The Dagger	151
La cama	152
The Bed	153
Nacer nacer	154

To Be Born To Be Born	155
Está	156
Is	157
Envolturas	158
Wrappings	159
Par impar	160
Even Odd	161
Pelícanos	162
Pelicans	163
¿Qué se sabe?	164
What Do You Know?	165
Distribuciones	166
Distributions	167
Interrupciones	168
Interruptions	169
Velocidades	170
Velocities	171
La muchacha	172
The Girl	173
La foto	174
The Photo	175
Ecco	176
Ecco	177
Caminos	178
Paths	179
Nieblas	180
Mists	181
Reflexiones	182
Reflections	183
Novedades	184
Novelties	185

Espera	186
Wait	187
Juegos	188
Games	189
Pérdidas	190
Losses	191
Callar	192
To Silence	193
A saber	194
To Wit	195
Exposiciones	196
Expositions	197
Caramba	198
Caramba	199
Gran lástima sería	200
A Great Shame It Would Be	201
Cortesías	202
Courtesies	203
El otro	204
The Other	205
Paulina	206
Paulina	207
Hechos	208
Facts	209
Doble	210
Double	211
No ser sabe	212
Not Being Knows	213
Alambres	214
Wires	215
Dice	216

Says	217
A veces	218
At Times	219
Sirenas	220
Sirens	221
Tal vez	222
Perhaps	223
Cifras	224
Ciphers	225
La sed	226
The Thirst	227
Estaba	228
Was	229
Árboles	230
Trees	231
La espiral	232
The Spiral	233
Semillas	234
Seeds	235
Mendigos	236
Beggars	237
Así, así	238
So, So	239
Descubrimientos	240
Discoveries	241
Neblinas	242
Hazes	243
Translator's Note	245

Acknowledgements

We would like to thank Juan Gelman for asking us to translate *To World*; a privilege, a challenge, and an invaluable experience; and Mara La Madrid for her support in the endeavor.

An earlier version of the introduction appeared in *Los Angeles Review of Books* on March 23, 2014.

Juan Gelman: "There are hungers/ in the broken savor of the world"

When we last saw Juan Gelman on the morning of January 12 2014, just 48 hours before his passing, it didn't seem like death was near. He was noticeably frail, but he enthusiastically rang a tiny bell to call his nurse. He spoke in whispers, but with precision and clarity. In his wheelchair, a poncho covering his shoulders, a blanket covering his legs, he was dignity personified. He gave us a solemn report on his health: the relentless anemia, the beginnings of lung cancer. He explained his decision to hold out from home, to not go through with chemotherapy. He was well aware of everything, including the present translation of *To World* into English, which he had personally requested when the book came out in 2008. The conversation never once slipped through his fingers, and as always, his great wit was ever present. He even spoke of Cervantes, one of the captivity narratives, where he'd found some excellent verses. He offered us coffee, served in lovely china cups, and we gladly accepted. Mexico City's winter light filtered through every cranny of his apartment in Colonia Condesa. We were sure of his determination to fight for his life.

Juan Gelman, the most read, influential, and renowned Latin American poet of our times, published more than 30 books of poetry and won countless awards including the Cervantes Prize (2007), the top literary honor in Spanish-language literature. He worked as a journalist and translator, spent many years exiled in Europe and Latin America, and remained an ardent critic of Argentina's military dictatorship throughout his life. He was above all faithful to poetry as a transformative act, as the quest for a more humane society, as a way to broaden our understanding of the world, as the possibility of a universal dialogue. The Argentine writer Julio Cortázar said that Gelman's work must be read "by remaining open, allowing meaning to enter other doorways than those of syntactical structure," for "only in this way can the reader discover the reality of the poems, which is none other than the exact and literal reality of the horror and death, but also the hope, that define Argentina" (qtd. in Gelman, *Unthinkable* 4). Gelman's death marks the end of an era in poetry written in Spanish characterized by Saúl Yurkievich as "uniting the cutting edge of both politics and art in one common cause," where poets strove "to say all that is sayable, though never alienating the poetic sign's specific necessities, knowing above all that it is a verbal occurrence subject to its own processes," which they aimed "to make use of and advance" (153).[1]

Juan Gelman was born in Buenos Aires, in 1930, and grew up like any other working-class porteño, devoted to soccer and milonga, in the Villa Crespo neighborhood. It stuck with him; he never forgot he was part of a family of Jewish immigrants from the Ukraine—an Argentine underdog until the very end. His brother Boris, often reciting Pushkin to him in Russian, was his first intellectual inspiration, introducing him to the works of Hugo, Dostoyevsky, and Tolstoy, as well as to other modern and contemporary classics. He was a precocious writer; at the age of 11 he published his first poem in the anarchist journal *Rojo y negro*. At the time, the concept of writing workshops didn't exist, but even if it had, he would have refused to participate. For him, "the only way you learn poetry is from reading poets, above all the greats" (Rodríguez Núñez 151). He was, however, a defender of dialogue among poets and ideological coincidences, and so in the 50s, along with other young, rebellious writers, he founded the poetry group *El Pan Duro*. He was discovered soon after by Raúl González Tuñón, one of the major voices of the Argentine poetic avant-garde, who celebrated in the young poet's work "an intense, sharp lyricism coupled with notably social content, and yet still open to the pleasures of the imagination," characteristic of a true artist's consciousness where "there will always be an inalienable, uncrushable domain" (qtd. in Boccanera 25).

---

[1] All translations from the Spanish are our own, unless otherwise noted.

In Gelman's first poetic cycle, made up of *Violín y otras cuestiones* (1949–1956), *El juego en que andamos* (1957–1958), *Velorio del solo* (1959–1961), *Gotán* (1962), and the vast majority of *Cólera buey* (1962–1968), what abounds is a neo-realist poetics and the search to establish a connection with the reader.[2] Generally speaking, it is a critical affirmation of the Latin American avant-garde's revolutionary poetic discourse. The poetry challenges the neo-colonial condition along with modernity's characteristic individualism, and questions both oppressive social realities and redeeming revolutionary ideals, but does not neglect forms of aesthetic representation. This is achieved by thoroughly revising realism, above all, through the use of the distancing effect. Gelman's work doesn't try to trap the reader in an illusory world of reality; instead, poems break with the automatic perception of things and facts. He intentionally makes no effort to hide the signifier, the sign, in his poetry, such that we not limit our focus to just the signified, the referent. As for the search for communication with the reader, Gelman's poetry does not aspire to be understood by everyone, instead what's emphasized is the implicit message—which leads to the reader being co-author of the text. Thus, it rejects the authoritative monologue and the usurpation of the other's voice, and privileges the values and the language of the streets, but without the fanaticism often associated with such a move, as well as the lexicon of the social sciences.

All this becomes apparent in a poem like "Heroes":

suns sun and seas sea
pharmacists prescribe
dictate beautiful scripts for pathosis
breakfast in their great centimeter

it's my turn to gelman

---

[2] To date, none of these books has been published in its entirety in English translation. Selections appear in *Dark Times Filled with Light* (Trans. Hardie St. Martin. Rochester: Open Letter, 2012.)

we've lost our fear of the great horse
successive hatchets befall us
and it forever dawns in testicles

it's a big deal for this to happen
considering love's badhand these days
decks of catastrophes debts
may those who hate be loved

children who eat at the hands of my livers
and their disgrace and grace is not being blind
the great mother horse
the great father horse

the world is a horse
time to gelman time to gelman i tell them
time to meet the most beautiful ones
those who prevailed with their great defeat (I 171)

Here, the poetic subject opposes oppression and repression, their "successive hatchets," and aligns himself with those who seek radical social change. Yet, at the same time, he demands his own personal agency with the call "to gelman" and affirms poetry's creativity as an alternative way of knowing.

With the work of Juan Gelman and his contemporaries—including Jorgenrique Adoum (Ecuador), Enrique Lihn (Chile), Fayad Jamís (Cuba), Juan Calzadilla (Venezuela), Roque Dalton (El Salvador), José Emilio Pacheco (Mexico), and Antonio Cisneros (Peru), among others—Spanish American poetry became a dialogic discourse. And this discourse turned even more radical in the Argentine's next poetic cycle, with the final sections of *Cólera buey*—"Traducciones I: Los poemas de John Wendell (1965–1968)" and "Traducciones II: Los poemas de Yamanokuchi Ando (1968)," along with the books *Traducciones III: Los poemas de Sidney West* (1968–1969) and *Fábulas*

(1970–1971).³ These texts highlight the use of translation and narrativity, though they never shift to the epic and remain firmly in the lyrical, drawing them closer to the magic realism of Gabriel García Márquez, and undoubtedly allowing for the creation of an intertwining of voices, a greater democracy within representation. The stories narrated in *Los poemas de Sidney West*, a supposed translation of an American poet, work as instances of the dehumanization of Argentina's deformed, dependent modernity. During a conversation in 2007, we asked Gelman where all these characters, their names and stories had come from. He confessed, "I'd closed myself off in a kind of intimism. [...] So I thought I'd make up some poets to see if I could get going again. And then they appeared, one was English, one Japanese, and the other American [...]. These poets were definitely not me. It all came from my imagination, the names and the situations" (Rodríguez Núñez 154–155).

In the first half of the 70s, while Octavio Paz—one of the key voices of Latin American post-avant-garde poetry, along with José Lezama Lima (Cuba), Nicanor Parra (Chile), and Alberto Girri (Argentina)—proclaimed for Latin American letters the end of "that tradition which seeks continuity through rejection" (102) beginning with Romanticism and concluding with the Avant-garde, and so the fall of the "notion of future as well as that of change" (158), Juan Gelman came out with *Relaciones* (1971 and 1973). Upon close reading of this book, along with *Hechos* (1974–1978), one sees not only a chronological continuity, as together they cover almost the entire decade of the 70s, but also a unity of content, along with very few formal differences between them. What Ana María Porrúa observed in *Relaciones*, that "it is a book on writing and its ties to reality" (65), could also be said about *Hechos*. Both encapsulate a new poetic cycle for Gelman, ever reluctant to remain idle, that continues to distance itself both from romanticism by questioning the poetic I, and from

---

3   *The Poems of Sidney West* is the only collection from this cycle that has appeared in its entirety in English. It was the first book to come out in this same series with Salt Publishing (Cambridge, 2009). Selections from these books as well as many others have appeared in *Unthinkable Tenderness* and *Dark Times Filled with Light*.

realism by emphasizing the auto-referentiality of language.

Jorge Fondebrider writes that *Hechos* "implies a change in Gelmanian poetics. The narrative poems almost completely disappear; verses suffer internal fracturing, denoted by an exasperated use of slashes. Gelman folds over onto himself and writes from the basis of absolute reflection;" here "what matters to him is presenting his own perception of what's real" (26). The aptly-titled "Ars Poetica" illustrates the transformation in poetics, a rupturing of both content and form:

> like a hammer reality/hammers away
> at the membranes of the soul or the heart/forges on
> in heat or in cold/presumes nothing/dries out
> the rotten illusions/thinks
>
> like a hoarse-voiced bird/raves
> in its dreams/roars the roar
> of Pascual's tiger/stomps on
> the little membranes of the soul or the heart/sizzled
>
> in your heat tomorrow/will sound
> like a shot in the forehead of the compañero who died yesterday
> and in what has yet to die and be born/
> like a hammer (*Unthinkable* 19)

Beforehand Fondebrider had pointed out the core poems in *Relaciones*, "which interrogated writing. The latter is brilliantly questioned: does the idea of transcendence matter for writing? What about the I as a poem's motive? What is the real commitment a writer has to literature?" (25). As for us, beyond the above-mentioned formal differences, which mostly appear beginning with *Notas* (1979), in *Relaciones* there is no less a reflection on reality than in *Hechos*, nor less reflection on writing in *Hechos* than in *Relaciones*. Both books are eminently reflective and the reflection is deeply personal.

At that time, Gelman's life and work were facing their most difficult moment. "Then came military dictatorships, civil governments, and new military dictatorships; they took away my books, my bread, my son, they made my mother despair, they threw me out of the country, killed my brothers, tortured my comrades [. . .]" (I 623). From a young age, Gelman had been a hardworking political activist and a critical journalist. He was forced into exile for 13 years by the military dictatorship that laid waste to Argentina from 1976 to 1983, and the corrupt governments to follow. In 1976, the far right kidnapped his children, Nora Eva, 19, and Marcelo Ariel, 20, along with the latter's wife, María Claudia Iruretagoyena, 19, who was seven months pregnant. Nora Eva would later reappear, but his son and daughter-in-law were eventually murdered, their child born in a concentration camp. The desperate search for the truth about his family's whereabouts culminated in the appearance of his granddaughter Macarena in Uruguay in 2000, transforming Juan Gelman into one of the most relevant symbols of the struggle for human rights.

The situation became the source of a new phase in his work, where he transformed the deepest sorrow into some of his best poetry: *Notas* (1979), *Carta abierta* (1980), *Si dulcemente* (1980), *Comentarios* (1978–1979), *Citas* (1979), *Hacia el sur* (1981–1982), *Bajo la lluvia ajena (notas al pie de una derrota)* (1980), *La junta luz* (1982), *Com/posiciones* (1984–1985), *Eso* (1983–1984), *Anunciaciones* (1985), and *Carta a mi madre* (1984–1987).[4] In *Carta abierta*, for instance, a poem/letter written to his disappeared son, the poetic subject adopts gender markings contradictory to those ordered by social norms:

with head hung low my burning soul

---

4   *Carta abierta*, *Comenatarios*, *Citas*, and *Com/posiciones* are available in English translation (*Between Words: Juan Gelman's Public Letter* (2010), *Commentaries and Citations* (2010), and *Com/positions* (2013), Trans. Lisa Rose Bradford. San Francisco: Coimbra Editions.) *Carta a mi madre* [*Letter to My Mother*] appears in *Pinholes in the Night: Essential Poems from Latin America*. Trans. Katherine M. Hedeen and Víctor Rodríguez Núñez. Sel. Raúl Zurita. Ed. Forrest Gander. Port Townsend: Copper Canyon, 2014.

dips a finger in your name/scrawls
your name on the walls of night/
amounting to nothing/solemnly bleeding/

soul to soul she watches you/enkindlering/
opens her mother chest to cuddle you/
shelter you/reunite you/undie you/
tiny shoe of yours taking its first steps upon

the world's sufferingblock tendering it/
clarity trodden/water undone
since you speak so/you crackle/burn/want/
give me your nevers like a true blue boy (*Between* 41)

A feminism stands out here as the poem renounces traditional norms of paternity, privileging certain qualities normally reserved for maternity, especially tenderness. In the selection above, the lyrical voice is transformed into a soul (feminine in Spanish and represented as "she" in the second stanza), who cuddles, shelters, reunites and undies. As for form, the process of inverting the mother and father's social roles takes shape through a profusion of diminutives ("tiny shoe"), an abundance of neologisms ("enkindlering" and "tendering"), and changes in the grammatical gender of nouns ("mother chest"). In this way, Gelman redefines the relationship between father and son, implying the de/construction of the masculine gender and the construction of a more inclusive lyrical voice, a move that brings with it serious social and cultural implications in favor of women's emancipation.

The constant innovation characteristic of Juan Gelman's poetry up until this point became even more accentuated in his work's last cycle, which included *Salarios del impío* (1984–1992), *Dibaxu* (1983–1985), *Incompletamente* (1993–1995), *Valer la pena* (1996–2000), *País que fue será* (2001–2004), *Mundar* (2004–2007), *De atrásalante en su porfía* (2007–2009), *El emperrado corazón amora* (2010), and *Hoy* (2013).[5] In

---

5 The present edition of *To World* is the only collection from this last cycle

Dibaxu we find the only prologue Gelman wrote for his own books. Here he tells his readers he envisioned the text "in Ladino"—clarifying that he is "of Jewish origin, but not Sephardic"—and that something got lost in his own translation of it into Spanish. Likewise, he emphasizes the book's continuity with his prior work, since he considered these poems as "the outfall of *Citas* and *Comentarios* [. . .] whose texts are in dialogue with the Spanish of the sixteenth century." More importantly, he explains the reasons behind it: "It was as if the extreme solitude of exile were pushing me to find my roots in language; the deepest, most exiled roots of language." And their consequences: "Ladino syntax gave me back its diminutives and a lost candor, a tenderness from another time that lives on, and is, consequently, filled with solace" (II 199).

Díbaxu's content is multidimensional, but in the end, its very core is positively charged with love:

morning makes the birds shimmer/
it's open/has freshness/
we'll drink it along
with the fear of thought/

sweetheart:
heat up what's past/
say kisses and the kisses will awaken/
we'll fall near the sun/

I recalled your blushing petticoats/
your blushing flowers/
your blushing kisses/
your heart white/ (II 203)

His approach to the subject is exemplary; as Carlos Monsiváis notes, "Gelman's force feeds on the absence of melodramatic

---

to be translated and published in English. Selections from *Salarios del impío* appear in *Dark Times Filled with Light*.

gestures" (20). Yet in *Dibaxu*, what truly changes is the form, it's absolutely singular experimental character—when it achieves a negation of negations, a critical affirmation of tradition. And it's not only because it was written in an ancient, minority, oppressed language, or because the questions, which had tenaciously crisscrossed all of Gelman's verse ever since *Relaciones*, had diminished. In the book's "Scholium" the author himself made it evident, "[p]erhaps this book is scarcely a reflection on language from its most charred corner, poetry" (II 199). For the poetic subject the power of enunciation is limitless and comes from the other. In love's alterity lies the possibility of knowledge. Poetry is nothing if not dialogue, confluence.

As for *Salarios del impío*, an epigraph by Euripides reveals the key to its innovative content, "the penalty for an impious man" is not "a swift death," but to die "a wanderer from your ancestral land over foreign soil." (II 183). Once more, we are faced with the same sorrow, both personal and collective, but this time it's thought through more deliberately. The poetry is unusual, active contemplation where intervention isn't always successful, yet pessimism never gains the upper hand. The uniqueness of the book is striking, including its poetic form, mostly made up of very short prose poems like "To Say":

> Journeys, faces, vicious tobacco, check stub animals, finger held in fear, the good of handkerchiefs, visits of nothingness, the tiny mirror of knowing, the mornings with child murmur, the fetus of the night, so much lamb tethered to thread, and patiences, patiences like fire, and you.
> You. (II 191)

It's worth mentioning that in Gelman's work the prose poem is present from the very beginning, from *Violín y otras cuestiones* on into books from different phases, like *Cólera buey*, *Eso*, and *Bajo la lluvia ajena*. Yet what prevails in those collections is a direct language, and in *Salarios del impío*, a much greater tropological density is revealed.

Questions only pop up in a few poems; unlike *Dibaxu*, now the slashes have disappeared and upper-case letters and punctuation marks are incorporated.

In 1997 Juan Gelman published *Incompletamente*, a book where "the abstract violin sounds" with perfect pitch (II 242). The speculation here undoubtedly has its roots in "the ruins of the moment," the political defeat of progressive forces in Argentina (II 257). The warnings against "oblivionation" still echo, the lyrical voice still clutches "his tiny borrowed bones!" (II 232). At the start of the book is a proverb taken from the Judeo-Spanish tradition, "The living cannot take up the tasks of the dead." Accordingly, the dead are irreplaceable, they carry out certain functions, they are active. Suffering is the reason behind this poetry, yet wisely it is not limited to only an expression of suffering. Generally speaking, in Gelman's later poetics, intellect triumphed over feeling; out of any action, the most relevant is thinking. For Monsiváis, the "ferociously political poet" complements this "metaphysical inquirer" (11). Still, once more, it has nothing to do with a traditional contemplative attitude. Reason is not privileged as it "stockpiles its blindness" somewhere and the poetic subject acts "with a madman's lucidity." Dream, "its too much seeing" (II 250), takes center stage.

Indeed, as Eduardo Milán notes, Juan Gelman "has doubted practically everything, but he's never doubted poetry" (12). *Incompletamente*'s poetic speaker ultimately strives to be brought back to life through words. This is not, however, an individual choice, but a social one, since "what's yours is not what you are" (II 264). Poetry is tellingly (in class terms) referred to as a "baker," and is honored for its vital purpose: "you shine so no one has to suffer!" (II 231–32). Hope remains, at whatever cost. With respect to form, *Incompletamente* is another major turning point in Gelman's poetics. As in earlier books, poems go untitled, only lower-case letters are used, and except for question and exclamation marks, punctuation is rejected, replaced by slashes. The change arises in the vast majority of the poems having 14 verses, grouped in two stanzas of four and two of three; the association with the sonnet is unavoidable.

The absence of rhyme and the use of free verse make it quite apparent that we're before an innovative appropriation of the traditional poetic form:

> THE DESOLATED light has no
> memory or project/heads
> toward its loss account/won't stop
> in its allusion to the dog/to the child/to
>
> the awful certainty/knocks
> on the doors of limit/sinks
> into the placenta of quivering smoke
> which causes it rages of existence/is
>
> astonished/removes
> ruins from its not being/chases
> the all-bearing blindness/
>
> what about the dream sound
> in the slums of sorrow?/
> the earth wrecked from disaster? (II 239)

Once again the poet's "expressive quest, both unyielding and tireless" shines through (Milán 15–16).

To World holds a distinguished place in the last phase of Juan Gelman's poetry, a touchstone that includes *De atrásalante en su porfía*, *El emperrado corazón amora*, and *Hoy*. It is uncompromisingly built upon the principal aim of this art: to be a way of thinking. The poems interrogate everything: nature, society, and thought itself, with no prejudice or even principle. In other words, they don't follow any rule, tradition, or discipline; they are decidedly critical. One could affirm here, like in any true manifestation of the genre, that poetry acts as an anti-ideology. Thought is not reduced to philosophical, ethical, religious, political, or aesthetic interpretations.

Rather, we are before thought in its totality, unwilling to recognize borders—although never in a pure state, not falling into speculation, into thinking just for thinking's sake. Furthermore, thought is always related to experience, both personal and collective, and above all, emotion. It never once stops being thought through image, that is to say, lyrical.

Beginning with the junction that is *To World*—a verb created by Gelman that might be defined as the register of reality's resonance, though it does not imply renouncing knowledge of the thing itself—his poetry seems to be stripped of any formal adornments. Only occasionally does he appeal to devices that are undoubtedly trademarks, like verbal invention, the use of slashes and prose poems, and the lack of punctuation and upper-case letters. Nonetheless, the question, the poetic device he is perhaps best known for, is never abandoned; it's the basis for the interpellation of reality; Gelmanian poetics through and through. The book is made up of 112 poems of varying size, that never goes beyond a page. Verses are, in general, less than 14 metric syllables long, and are characterized by constant enjambment. Language is not affected but quotidian, yet it does sometimes spiral around itself to arrive at the borders of a baroque style. This poetry speaks of poetry; it takes it all on: the objective and subjective, the real and imagined, I and other. It ventures into virgin territory, on the outskirts of romanticism, realism, symbolism, and the avant-garde, where others will surely go.

Gelman's poetry is a model of rebelliousness and freedom, a lesson in devotion and rigor, and it places him among the greatest poets in the Spanish language. He's a direct descendent of Rubén Darío, Antonio Machado, César Vallejo, Vicente Huidobro, Federico García Lorca, Pablo Neruda, and José Lezama Lima. It would be particularly amiss if we didn't stress how he challenged the dogmas of revolutionary writing. He put into practice, while at the same time questioning, a poetics that reaffirmed poetry's ability to grasp—in its historicity, in its contradictory character, and in its diversity—natural and social phenomena. He envisioned poetic writing, without lessening its essential condition as a creative practice, as an instrument both to interpret and to transform reality. And he continues to be the ideal of a poet mindful of his ties to nature and society, who makes every effort to join the political avant-garde and the aesthetic avant-garde—art and life. The influence of such a poetic practice, its backing of the right to imagination and faithfulness to feeling, has been crucial for poets from later generations.

Juan Gelman lived the last two decades of his life in Mexico, where he easily became an essential part of its cultural life, and it's where he chose to die. As he had wanted, his ashes were scattered in a garden in Neplanta, the small town where the first great Spanish language poet in America, Sor Juana Inés de la Cruz, was born. He frequently traveled to Argentina, where he had family, friends, and a legion of readers. The government there declared three days of national mourning when he died. The news of his death was in all the important international papers, which offered their deepest sympathies, though they had consistently refused to publish the anti-imperialist articles he wrote tirelessly throughout his life. He continued to write them until his body finally gave out, each piece a model of informative accuracy and intellectual analysis. Those critical articles, among other things, banned his travel to the United States, and consequently his receiving an honorary degree from Kenyon College. Surely they scared off the Swedish academics too, just as Jorge Luis Borges' commentaries of a different political nature had done, and so Argentina has been denied—for the second time—a well-deserved Nobel Prize.

KATHERINE M. HEDEEN and VÍCTOR RODRÍGUEZ NÚÑEZ
Gambier-Palo Alto, May, 2014

Works Cited

Benedetti, Mario. *Los poetas comunicantes*. 2nd. ed. Mexico: Marcha Editores, 1981.

Boccanera, Jorge. *Confiar en el misterio: Viaje por la poesía de Juan Gelman*. Buenos Aires: Sudamericana, 1994.

Euripides. *Hippolytus*. Trans. David Kovacs. Cambridge: Harvard UP, 1995. http://www.perseus.tufts.edu/hopper/text?doc=Perseus%3Atext%3A1999.01.0106%3Acard%3D1021

Fondebrider, Jorge. Introduction. *Antología poética*. By Juan Gelman. Ed. Fondebrider. Buenos Aires: Espasa Calpe, 1994. 13–31.

Gelman, Juan. *Poesía reunida*. 2 vols. Buenos Aires: Seix Barral, 2012.

———. *Between Words: Juan Gelman's Public Letter*. Trans. Lisa Rose Bradford. San Francisco: Coimbra Editions, 2010.

———. *Unthinkable Tenderness*. Trans. and Ed. Joan Lindgren. Berkeley: U of California P, 1997.

Milán, Eduardo. "Prólogo". *Pesar todo: Antología*. By Juan Gelman. Havana: Casa de las Américas, 2003. 7–17.

Monsiváis, Carlos. "Juan Gelman: ¿Y si Dios dejara de preguntar?" *Otromundo: Antología 1956–2007*. Mexico: FCE, 2008. 9–24.

Paz, Octavio. *Children of the Mire*. Trans. Rachel Phillips. Cambridge. Harvard UP, 1991.

Porrúa, Ana María. "*Relaciones* de Juan Gelman: El cuestionamiento de las certezas poéticas." *Revista de Crítica Literaria Latinoamericana* 35 (1992): 61–70.

Rodríguez Núñez, Víctor. "Juan Gelman: Poesía es interrogación." *La poesía sirve para todo*. Havana: Unión, 2008. 149–161.

Yurkievich, Saúl. *La confabulación con la palabra*. Madrid: Taurus, 1978.

Through that holy sound,
which all creation echoes

HILDEGARD OF BINGEN (1098–1179)

La manzana

Manzana sola en la fuente,
¿qué hace sin Paraíso? Nadie ve
su cicatriz amarga.
¿Me pregunta
a dónde fue el secreto
de irse por tanta puerta
cerrada, alto el crepúsculo
firme, la cara que
sueña, sueña, sueña,
sin importar lo que perdió?
En un rincón, el viento
mueve la sombra de las hojas.

The Apple

Lone apple on the platter,
what's it doing with no Eden? No one
glimpses its bitter scar.
Is it asking me
where the secret to parting
through so many closed
doors has gone, the high, steady
twilight, the face
dreaming, dreaming, dreaming,
with no regard for what it lost?
In a corner, the wind
rustles the shadow of the leaves.

Compañeros

En una casa para locos
vi lo ocurrido todavía.
Las páginas del dolor esquivado
en las mejillas del ausente.
Un árbol se parece allí
al espanto que no
espera ni una piedra. Los que aúllan
con imágenes tristes
lindan con un perro que muere.
El instante del agua solar
está muy lejos de la mano. Los
compañeros en la dilación
crean charcos
con los ojos nomás.

Comrades

In a madhouse
I saw what happened still.
The pages of ache dodged
on the cheeks of the absentee.
There a tree resembles
the fear not even
expected by a stone. Those who howl
with sad images
border on a dying dog.
The instant of solar water
is far from hand. The
comrades in the delay
form puddles
from their eyes only.

El pato salvaje

En medio de su olvido ocurre
la grandeza del mundo en la
fuga del pato salvaje.
Y cómo vuela la criatura, cómo
escribe trecho a trecho fuego
en la forma invisible
que apuesta contra él.
Eso es volar y los espacios
de lo que triste era, rocan
un todo pequeñito.
Ave pájaro que
cruzás el cielo como una ilusión
de lo que fue no sido
bajo el sol que no hace preguntas.

A Jorge Boccanera

The Wild Duck

Amid its oblivion befalls
the greatness of the world in the
wild duck's fleeing.
And how the creature flies, how
it writes fire from stretch to stretch
on the invisible shape
that wagers against it.
This is flying and the spaces
of what was sad boulder
a tiny whole.
Bird fowl you
cross the sky like an illusion
of what was not been
beneath the unquestioning sun.

To Jorge Boccanera

Amistades

El poema que estaba en la cabeza
del corazón se fue. Esto habla
de la certidumbre de la incertidumbre
que nadie puede medir.
Tu brazo nada
en el temblor del sucedido.
¿Qué caballos
te recaballan la nación
de las ausencias que buscás
en la ausencia de vos? Es la amistad
del todo con la nada, la
del pecho mismo con
su perdón, sus espejos,
no dormir.

Friendships

The poem in the head
of the heart has left. This speaks
to the certainty of uncertainty
no one can measure.
Your arm swims
in the trembling of what's taken place.
What horses
rehorse your nation
of the absences you seek
in the absence of you? It's the friendship
of all with nothing, the
very chest with
its pardon, its mirrors,
no sleeping.

Escondrijos

El envión de la palabra la
lleva al borde que no
puede cruzar. Gime ahí
como una grulla loca,
un desperdicio del destino.
La saludo, la amo cuando
se instala como cuerpo en
mi cuerpo contra
la piel del día, las
sombras que se agitan
en escondrijos de la juventud
como si fueran de verdad.

A *Carlos Monsiváis*

Hideaways

The shove of the word it
carries it to the edge it
cannot go over. It groans there
like a mad crane,
a squandering of destiny.
I greet it, I love it when
it settles in like a body in
my body against
the day's skin, the
shadows stirring
in hideaways of youth
as if they were real.

To Carlos Monsiváis

La alondra

El que vuelve a sí mismo pasa
por la calle agarrado a
lo que no ocupa.
Se fue el saber a su ignorancia en
la tarde sin parientes
de la desolación. Hay un recuerdo
mordido por la alondra
que no voló por mi garganta.
Sube entre el espejo y el ojo
un día claro del fondo desierto.

The Lark

One returning to himself goes
down the street clutched to
what doesn't occupy.
Wisdom left for its ignorance in
the evening with no kin
to desolation. There's a memory
bitten by the lark
that didn't fly through my throat.
Amid mirror and eye rises
a clear day from the deserted backdrop.

Debajo

Crujen las cartas que nunca te escribí.
Matan al perro
en mi memoria siempre.
¿Quién le da de comer? La
anticipación de la mañana
talla tu rostro en mí. Respirás
a mi lado. En los agujeros
de lo que toca vivir hay
la marea del tiempo, lleva
dolores a su basura inútil. El sudor
del pasado golpea
su páramo roto, la
vida continua, los
pensamientos con plomo debajo.

A Mara

Below

The letters I never wrote to you crackle.
They always kill the dog
in my memory.
Who feeds it? The
expectation of morning
etches your face on me. You breathe
by my side. In the holes
of what we must live there's
time's tide, it carries
aches away to its worthless rubbish. The sweat
of the past striking
its severed moor, the
continuous life, the
thoughts with lead below.

To Mara

Ahí

No verse es mirar un árbol
que olvidó. ¿Quién dijo
que en el olvido nada
puede crecer? Brotan ahí
las desesperaciones de
un mundo murmurado, inquilino
de abismos donde
el más allá del sol es un
piano que nadie toca.

There

To not see yourself is to watch a tree
that forgot. Who said
nothing can grow
in oblivion? There bloom
the desperations of
a murmured world, tenant
of abysses where
the sun's hereafter is a
piano no one plays.

Accidentes

En las migas de tu esplendor,
mamá, recibí el recital
de pogroms y de sangre
que dio rostro a mi rostro.
El puente de esas vidas es
lo respirado a cuestas.
Desde tus hombros miro
las arrugas de las estrellas célebres.
A un dedo de lo que fui me soy
en lo que habré de ser. Tanto mundo,
tanta abierta confianza en su cambiar
el accidente,
desastres que
dicen al lado adiós.

Accidents

In the crumbs of your splendor,
mama, I received the recital
of pogroms and blood
that gave a face to my face.
The bridge of those lives is
the breathed on our backs.
From your shoulders I watch
the wrinkles of celebrated stars.
A finger's length from what I was I am
in what I must be. So much world,
so much open trust in its altering
the accident,
disasters
bidding farewell nearby.

La conversación con Mara esta noche

La piedra de la palabra
es un cuerpo solo.
Vino la mano del amor
que se besa en los puentes.
¿Estás ahí, peligro
de la frente que pasa sin soñar?
Cada sombra captura un rostro
de su sombra. No hay mástiles
en el vacío que se ahoga con
qué furor este día.
Soltá tu espanto, derribá
las malas cifras de la bruma.
El deseo del mantel de lino
brilla en la oscuridad.

The Conversation with Mara Tonight

The stone of the word
is a lone body.
The hand of love
kissed on bridges came.
Are you there, threat
of the brow to pass by dreamless?
Every shadow captures a face
of its shadow. There are no masts
in the void drowning with
so much furor today.
Let loose your fear, topple
the bad ciphers of the brume.
The linen tablecloth's desire
glows in the darkness.

Líneas

La parálisis del duelo no
sale a la calle. Dura
hacia adelante, hacia atrás. La
dulce noche
es una línea del paisaje que
indescifrable canta. El tiempo,
¿es demasiado en
esta isla de fuego
que no se quiere apagar?
La miro como
si no estuviera ahí, pensando
en qué piensa, arrastrada
hacia el sur, como un pedazo del
sueño que preguntaba
por qué su lengua es un verano solo
en lo que va a venir.

Lines

Grief's paralysis doesn't
take to the streets. It lasts
forward, backward. The
sweet night
is a landscape line
indecipherably singing. Time,
is it too much on
this island of fire
that refuses to be snuffed out?
I watch it as
if it weren't there, thinking
about what's it thinking, dragged
toward the south, like a bit of the
dream that asked
why its tongue is a summer only
in what is to come.

Callejones

Los que respetan su ignorancia
merecen más cielo que
los acostados en un banco
que ráspaban con ira.
¿Se hace sola la doble conciencia
donde la huella brilla?
¿Por qué no creer en el sencillo
callejón de la espera?
Allí sustituyen al mundo
con el cantar del universo.
Canta y canta
para sacarnos de aquí.

Alleyways

Those who respect their ignorance
deserve more heaven than
those lying on a bench
they've scraped with rage.
Does double consciousness form itself
where the trace glows?
Why not believe in the wait's
simple alleyway?
There the world's swapped
for the universe song.
It sings and sings
to get us out of here.

Cosmos

El pan quemado recuerda a la boca
que no hable de los
carbones que encendió.
Hay parásitos, comen
del sufrimiento a otro, de
la pecho que cantaba, de
los vivos en la imaginación.
El animal del horizonte calla
sus abismos detrás.
El cosmos tiembla
como lo pájaro perdido
sin coartada.

Cosmos

The burnt bread reminds the mouth
not to speak of the
coals it lit.
There are parasites, they eat
from the suffering to another, from
the chest that sang, from
the living in imagination.
Horizon's animal silences
its abysses behind.
The cosmos trembles
like what's bird lost
with no alibi.

Tarde

Esta tarde se acuesta en
calles que caminé, me trae
su oro. Cuando
el pasado devuelve su pasado así
hay un oleaje de bocas que
mojan otra vez sombras
que ruegan por nosotros.
Unas viejas sentadas en la calle
hacen con suave náhuatl
el pasado de esta tarde contra
el frío de las casas desiertas.
El lenguaje va
a muros ciegos y
hay rostros que empiezan de nuevo.

Evening

This evening lies down on
streets I walked, brings me
its gold. When
the past returns its past like so
there's a swell of mouths
once more wetting shadows
that beg for us.
Some old women sitting on the street
with smooth Nahuatl make
this evening's past against
the chill of deserted houses.
The language goes off
to blind walls and
there are faces beginning anew.

El niño

El niño duerme
al pie de un árbol y el aire
que lo relata brilla
como vida en la vida, se vuelca
con claro alivio sobre
la piel llena de caminos, sube
en el fulgor del día
para darle fulgor y el otoño
quiere al niño que duerme
al pie del aire y el
espanto se va, corrido
por una voz
que nadie escucha todavía
en la marea de las huellas.

The Child

The child sleeps
at the foot of a tree and the air
recounting him glows
like life in life, spills
with clear relief over
the skin filled with paths, rises
in the day's brilliance
to give him brilliance and autumn
loves the child sleeping
at the foot of the air and the
fear vanishes, run off
by a voice
no one hears yet
in the tide of traces.

Lejanías

La mecánica del alma no
significa estar
adentro. Caminar, respirar, ver,
escuchar, los demás,
no significa estar afuera.
El dentrofuera es un temblor tardío
y está ahí:
en una lejanía
que mece con
palabras que vencieron al fuego.

Distances

The soul's mechanics doesn't
mean to be
inside. To walk, breathe, see,
listen, the others,
doesn't mean to be outside.
The insideoutside is a tardy trembling
and it's there:
in a distance
swaying with
words that defeated fire.

Alas

Ala.
A la herida.
Alar ido
al espanto
que separa a la voz del corazón.
El alano que alarga su altivez.
Alondra aquí metida por
caprichos de la gallina con el gallo.
Alazán que el alba ocupás,
¡alargame el amor y su signo
que se alcohola en mis entrañas!
¡Ella, con alfabetos no leídos,
alumbramé lo que resiste al pairo!
En el alféizar de los huérfanos
pregunta qué pasó
y alza la noche.

Wings

Wing.
To the wound.
Ho wl
from the fear
winnowing voice from heart.
The Alano swelling its swagger.
Woodlark wedged here from
hen's whims with rooster.
Sorrel occupying the dawn,
widen love and its sign
wining in my insides!
She with words unread,
illumines me what withstands in lying to!
On the orphans' windowsill
she asks what happened
and waxes the night.

Poema

El árbol detrás
de la ventana pasa, la tarde
se lleva al mundo y pasa, serpea
la vez que fui, corriente arriba
de un río ancho
que pasa. Voces que humedecieron
la sal del viento, ahora en esta
constelación que pasa.
El manto de los pájaros
y el tiempo con su canción muda.

Poem

The tree behind
the window passes by, the evening
carries off the world and passes by, twisting
and turning the time I was, upstream
from a wide river
passing by. Voices dampened
the salt of the wind, now in this
constellation passing by.
The veil of birds
and time with its mute song.

A ver

En la tarde de al lado vive
una vieja que pide para el pan.
Así se calla el universo
con esa piedra encima y
lo que hiere
del dulce amor. La
canción de las raíces es
atravesada parte a parte
por una piedra que tiró
la tarde de al lado con
la lejanía de los grillos
calcinada
en una boca grande abierta.

Let's See

In the evening next door lives
an old woman who begs for bread.
So the universe grows silent
with that stone to bear and
what it wounds
of sweet love. The
root song is
crossed end to end
by a stone thrown by
the evening next door with
the distance of crickets
charred
in a wide open mouth.

Roces

Y cómo el roce de un gorrión
te puede herir y el cuerpo
se pone de revés.
Han clausurado huesos
del niño por quién sabe. Un soplo
de cuchillo apagó
el mal sabido mar que pudo ser.
Se ahogan el rostro, los
espérames, el clavo
que te clavó de ojos cerrados
contra una lengua.
La tarde se va
de lo que quiso a lo que pudo.

Brushings

And how the brushing of a sparrow
can wound you and your body
turns inside out.
Who knows why the child's bones
have been brought to a close. A gust
of blade put out
the badly known sea that could be.
They're drowning, the face, the
waitformes, the nail
that nailed you with eyes closed
against a tongue.
The evening passes
from what it wanted to what it could.

La extranjera

La extranjera no sabe
que mi sangre es su casa, que
todo pájaro suyo
sólo ahí puede cantar y abrir
alas de su verano y se alza
como una sed de mundo
que no se puede apagar.
El pájaro encendido cuida
los huecos de la pérdida como
joyas que fueron sin remedio.
Canta allí, loco de luz, no renuncia
a sus monstruos.
La hora de los dioses
junta los pies y ese camino
en llamas.

A Mara

The Foreigner

The foreigner doesn't know
my blood is her home, that
only there every one of
her birds can sing and open
wings from her summer and rise
like a thirst for world
unquenchable.
The ignited bird cares for
the loss's hollows like
jewels that were hopelessly.
There it sings, crazy from light, doesn't forsake
her monsters.
The hour of gods
joins her feet and that path
in flames.

To Mara

Vienen cómo

Cargados de años, sí,
con verdes que fueron
y su fulgor a veces.
¿Dicen algo, dijeron algo
entonces? ¿Y a quién?
No traen
la piedra o el aliento
donde viví de mí.
El sol tiene un animal que no calma.
Pasaron muchos barcos
entre nosotros dos.

How They Come

Laden with years, yes,
with greens that were
and their brilliance at times.
Are they saying something? Did they
back then? And to whom?
They don't bear
the stone or breath
where I lived off me.
The sun has an animal unsettling.
Many ships passed
between the two of us.

Jardines

Los sentidos
reducen el jardín a su imagen,
lo retiran a una criatura que
entra en la sangre y vuela. Es
una alegría que no sabe
decir qué es. Calla
sobre las aulas del desierto,
su libro, ya.

Gardens

The senses
reduce the garden to its image,
diminish it to a creature
entering the blood and flying. It's
wonderful it doesn't know
how to say what it is. It silences
upon the desert's great halls,
its book, at last.

Islas

A ver:
un hombre y una mujer
viven en una isla asediada.
Los rodea el océano donde
ardió el plumaje de un jilguero
en el hilo del
amor que canta
en la espesura del vacío.
El jilguero los nombra y son
inseparables de sus nombres.
Los cerca el mundo como
un animal sin luz y cruel.
La tierra lame heridas
que hablan con ojos hacia adentro
y caen con
astros detrás.
A ver:
un hombre y una mujer
muerden las
envolturas marinas
de lo que amaron.

Islands

Let's see:
a man and a woman
live on an island besieged.
They are surrounded by the ocean where
a saffron finch's feathers burned
in the thread of
love singing
in the denseness of the void.
The finch names them and they are
inseparable from their names.
The world encloses them like
an animal lightless and cruel.
The earth licks wounds
that speak with eyes inward
and fall with
the astral behind.
Let's see:
a man and a woman
gnaw at the
sea wrappings
of what they loved.

La carta

Alguien llora la carta
que va a escribir. Afuera
se desmembrana el día en sus agüeros.
Una luz que viene de
millones de ojos que se juntan
y el vapor de la furia inmaculado
cambian las fechas de la muerte.
El fuego interior cuece
viejas iras para
que alguien les ponga nombre.

The Letter

Someone cries the letter
to be written. Outside
the day demembranes in its omens.
A light coming from
millions of eyes merged
and the immaculate steam of fury
change the dates of death.
The inner fire boils
old rages so
someone can name them.

Océanos

En el océano del vacío
hay nombres, nombres, nombres.
En el océano de lo perdido,
hay nombres.
¿Quién responde
a este chorro de alma
que los llama? Un oleaje
de nombres, nombres, nombres.
¿Qué los separa de la grande muerte
en brazos ya de lo que fueron?

Oceans

In the ocean of the void
there are names, names, names.
In the ocean of the lost,
there are names.
Who replies
to this soul stream
calling out to them? A swell
of names, names, names.
What separates them from the great death
now in the arms of what they were?

Regiros

en el regiro del catástrofe/pocos
sacaron alma/recovecos
de pásame la curva/lo que ya
pelaba crestas del gran sueño/o
pechaban contra
lo oscuro del ciclón/a ver/
escuchame la cara/¿huecos
de la pasión herida?/
¿a quién lo vieron luto?/está bueno
el álamo del amo/el
miedo que teje su revés
en el estruendo del callado/
pero no vengan con sus
casas de humo y mentira/
con lengua en púlpito a hablar/
sucios de sangre que se retiró/

Re-turns

in the re-turn of the catastrophe/few
showed their souls/hidden corners
of hand me the curve/what had already
plucked crests from the great dream/or
shouldered against
the dark of the cyclone/let's see/
listen to my face/hollows
of wounded passion?/
who had they seen mourning?/it's just fine
the proprietor's poplar/the
fear weaving it's underside
in the roar of the silent one/
but don't come around here with your
houses of smoke and lies/
with tongues at the pulpit when speaking/
dirty with blood re-treated/

Pasados

Pasado que pajara
su vida y muerte lo
lleva al otro de sí, a la creación
del animal angélico.
Se mueven alas del destino, son
cuerpos tocados por
zodíacos del barrio donde
la luz camina en el café.
Creció el horizonte de las
fugacidades que llevaba a pulso
algún sol interior.
Está maldito, pero
no lo echa a pique la maldad.
Tanto decir que se enmaraña mientras
la gran serpiente de alredor
quema universos.

Pasts

Past that birds
its life and death carries
it to the other of itself, to the creation
of the angelic animal.
Wings of destiny in motion, they're
bodies touched by
neighborhood zodiacs where
the light paces in coffee.
The horizon spread from the
fleetingnesses bearing freehand
some internal sun.
It's cursed, but
evil doesn't wreck it.
So much to say that it gets entangled while
the great serpent all a round
sets fire to universes.

Qué

¿Qué alegra la noche oscura? Una
palabra. ¿Qué
enalma la noche
oscura? Una palabra.
Una anchura del mundo.
Una palabra que
bebió sombras para brillar
ardiéndose. Un
polvo de astros toca
el enamor de una
palabra que
abriga el desgarrón.

What

What inspirits the dark night? A
word. What
insouls the dark
night? A word.
A breadth of the world.
A word that
swallowed shadows to glow
aflame. An
astral dusting caresses
the inlove of a
word that
shelters the gash.

Sacar

Sacar el pecho enfermo del pecho
es dar un viento nocturno que
se posa en las ramas
de lo que no va a ser. Se mueve
buscando resignación o paz, choca
contra las nieblas de la lengua
y hay palabras
con heridas mortales.
¡Oh dulces brazos que en sabor reposan!
Negra pedrada cayó ahí.
El preso de los ojos que ven
conoce urdimbres de serpientes.

To Draw Out

To draw out the ill chest from the chest
is to hand over a nocturnal wind
perching on the branches
of what won't be. It moves about
seeking resignation or peace, clashes
with the mists of the tongue
and there are words
with mortal wounds.
Oh sweet arms that in savor rest!
Black stoning fell there.
The prisoner with seeing eyes
knows serpent warps.

Hilos

El nudo ata hilos para que
no insistan en su pretensión
de coser.
El hilo calla y sigue con
el alma que le quieren atar.
Es el alma que le quieren atar
y
como amado en su amada desata
aires, aguas, ardores
que no se pueden apagar.
El nudo que ató la pobreza
es una cara de la nada.
Hay hambres
en el sabor roto del mundo.

Threads

The knot ties threads so
they won't insist on their intention
to sew.
The thread falls silent and keeps on with
the soul they want to tie to it.
It's the soul they want to tie to it
and
like a lover in his lover it loosens
winds, waters, warmths
powerless to be put out.
The knot tied by poverty
is a face of nothingness.
There are hungers
in the broken savor of the world.

El barranco

Voces al borde del barranco
llaman al niño que
hace señas
subiendo el día.
Crepita la canción y los
tratos de los sentidos andan
sin parte razonal.
El barranco
no vuelve a él sino a la furia
de su silencio.

The Barranca

Voices at the edge of the barranca
call out to the child who
makes signals
scaling the day.
The song crackles and the
dealings of the senses have
no reasonal share.
The barranca
doesn't turn to him but to the fury
of his silence.

Saludo

Querido Marco Antonio: Ella
seguirá visitando
tu enorme corazón. Allí se abriga
contra
las mordeduras de la época,
las guerras, la pobreza, los
malos poetas.
Con un fulgor de alma primera
te dejará para volver.
En los surcos abiertos por el dolor del mundo
te sembrará de vientos y
conocerá su rostro.

Greeting

Dear Marco Antonio, She'll
still visit
your enormous heart. There she's sheltered
against
the era's bitings,
the wars, the poverty, the
bad poets.
With a flash of first soul
she'll leave you to return.
In the furrows opened by the ache of the world
she'll sow you with winds and
know her face.

Soneto

Señora furia/¿por?/
¿por qué no la dejaron
solita y sola?/hay fuego/
fuego de sol/fuego de niños/

cortan la calle espesa de
furia/furias/el hielo
de su vejez/roto por la
caída de los llantos/¡oh dulce amor

que descansaba en la
suposición de rosas de agua!/
no primavera/no vigila

el callejón de las entrañas/
los tragos de la suerte/
el vuelo alto/

Sonnet

Madam fury/how?/
how come you weren't left
on your own and alone?/there's fire/
sun fire/children fire/

the street is cut thick with
fury/furies/the ice
of your old age/broken by the
fall of weeping/oh sweet love

that rested upon the
assumption of water roses!/
doesn't spring/ doesn't watch over

the alley of your insides/
the mouthfuls of fate/
flying high/

Paco

Apareció tu rostro en
una conversación. Yacías
en una conversación/tu
fulgor brillaba en una
conversación. Habrás
hablado mucho con tu muerte,
dos peces en el mar.
¿Qué hay por allí? ¿El puente de tu casa
donde pasaban ímpetus, sonora
la vida escrita en los
huesos de tu canción?
¿Hay perros, hay olvido ya?
Los veranos cuidaron tu congoja.
Nos vemos.

Paco

Your face appeared in
a conversation. You lay
in a conversation/your
brilliance glowed in a
conversation. You must've
talked a lot with your death,
two fish in the sea.
What's out there? The bridge by your house
where impulses crossed, sonorous
life written in the
bones of your song?
Are there dogs, is there oblivion by now?
The summers cared for your distress.
See you later.

La pregunta

La pregunta que no tiene respuesta
se convirtió en un sauce
verdísimo y todo su alredor
canta. Su entraña es
aire, también agua, pasado
de alguna luna que pasó.
En su madera más sutil
el tiempo lloró mucho.
Se apagaban los brazos,
los perros en el fondo,
ayes que no pudieron decir ay.

The Question

The question with no answer
changed to a deep green
willow and all a round it
sings. Its insides are
wind, water too, past
of some passed moon.
In its most subtle wood
time wept greatly.
They all faded away, the arms,
the dogs in the background,
ohs powerless to say oh.

Olvidos

¿Cómo de vos se olvida
mi amor por vos? ¿Ya no se quiere? ¿Busca
distancias, verse como
paisaje solamente?
¿Y qué será del canto
de suavidad que en lengua había?
¿Y cuándo ser nosotros
entregando ambas partes a
los párpados con noche?
Cuando tu mano es y cuando
tu voz con alma, el dolor
parece algo leído, un papel
arrugado y sin rostro
que ya vivió.

Oversights

How are you overlooked
by my love for you? Is it no longer fond of itself?
    Is it
bent on distances, seeing itself
only as landscape?
And what of the canto
of softness there was on tongue?
And when to be us
handing over both parts to
the eyelids with night?
When your hand is and when
your voice with soul, the ache
seems like something read, crumpled
faceless paper
that already lived.

Sucederá

Cuando alma y espíritu
y cuerpo sepan,
y la luna sea bella porque la amé
y el mundo esté parado al filo
de la memoria y
sangre la luz detrás
del baño de su gracia,
obligaremos al futuro
a volver otra vez. Allí
todos los ojos serán uno
y la palabra volverá a palabrear
contra sus criaturas.
Se acabará la eternidad y el poema
buscará todavía su
tripulación y lo
que no pudo nombrar, tan lejos.

It Will Happen

When soul and spirit
and body know,
and the moon's beautiful because I loved it
and the world's standing at the edge
of memory and
bleeds the light behind
the bathing of its grace,
we'll make the future
return once more. There
all eyes will be one
and the word will once more word
against its creatures.
Eternity will end and the poem
will still search out its
crew and what
it couldn't name, so far-off.

¿Cómo se llama?

la mano toca
la suavidad del monstruo/ése/
camina/te respira/
es antes de sí mismo/el mal
que retuerce los hígados/la cifra
que te volvió el alma otra/la
besada por mil vidas
en una sola floración/
la pluricaja del ausente/
las rotas de la música/se
consumieron las alas/nunca
volaron en el pañuelo verde/
bosques donde
lo encontrado es perdido/como
solazo que pendía
en lo despacio del dolor/

What's It Called?

the hand touches
the softness of the monster/that one/
walks/breathes you/
is before itself/the evil
twisting livers/the cipher
turned your soul into another/the
one kissed by a thousand lives
in one lone flowering/
the absentee's pluribox/
the music's broken ones /the
wings wasted away/they
never flew on the green scarf/
forests where
the found is lost/like
a scorching sun hung
in the slow of ache/

Tardes

La tarde está suave de
nacer en su morir y tu amor
la cruza como nave
en el estar donde encallamos
con sacos de la unión. ¿A dónde
se fue la paz que nunca hubo? Eso
absorbió agujureros. Tanta
pasión absorta en su pasión y los
registros del ciego de la época.
Cambió el hijo de rostro. Ahora
tiene una larga vida en el pesado
vuelo de mí hacia él, donde palabras
y pensamientos caen
en el hilo más corto.

Evenings

The evening's soft from
being born in its dying and your love
crosses it like a ship
in the passing where we run aground
with sacks from the joining. Where
did it go, the peace that never was? All that
absorbed pinholes. So much
passion absorbed in its passion and the
accounts of the era's blind man.
The son changed his face. Now
he has a long life in the heavy
flight from me toward him, where words
and thoughts fall
on the shortest thread.

Sépase

mientras te amo/un perro
ladra en la íntima cocina/
cosemos vida y muerte/
ojos puros tu mano/

¿a dónde se fue la canción/
de las canciones?/¿el
visible que munda en otra parte?/
¿abre el aire que no sucedió?/

¿estaba escrita la escritura
de dos en uno/la obra
que no conserva nada?/

nunca sabemos qué pasó/la noche
es nosotros/tranquila/
calla abismos/

Be It Known

while I love you/a dog
barks in the intimate kitchen/
we stitch life and death/
pure eyes your hand/

where did it go, the song/
of songs?/the
visible one who worlds elsewhere?
does the unhappened air open?/

was it written, the writing
of two in one/the work
that conserves nothing?/

we never know what took place/the night
is us/peaceful/
it silences abysses/

Albas

El alba
que va del mar a la colina
con la huella del color que pasó y
la memoria del color que tendrá
la quietud de la sangre,
cruza árboles delante del invierno,
trae la dicha y la desdicha
del nacido de un cuerpo.
Pero qué sol el sol que cae
y saca palabras de la tierra:
cosecha el vuelo indestructible
de los granos del sueño.
El aire del amor en la
mano que dibuja la muerte.

In memoriam Rapi Diego

Dawns

The dawn
spanning from sea to hill
with the trace of the color passed and
the memory of the color to be had
by blood's stillness,
crosses trees in the sight of winter,
bears the happiness and unhappiness
of the one born of a body.
Yet what sun the sun falling
and extracting words from the earth:
it harvests the indestructible flight
of the grains of dream.
The air of love in the
hand drawn by death.

In memoriam Rapi Diego

Patria

En la patria desnuda, al fondo
del fuego en
las casa de las palabras blancas,
un sol joven cesa
la vida de la muerte.
Lo que vendrá
le dejó huellas en la lengua.

A *Eduardo Hurtado*

Homeland

In the naked homeland, in the depths
of the fire in
the house of white words,
a young sun ceases
life from death.
What will come
left traces on its tongue.

To Eduardo Hurtado

Canción

Calentó el lecho
un pan caído en claridad,
arde el revés del día
en muchas diferencias.
Eso, no saber
nada, ser nada en el
océano de las manos perdidas.
Aquí y allá desordenadas las
fiestas del delirio,
el árbol donde paran
los crepúsculos. Hoy
viene mañana con ayer.
Se juntaron en un
viaje a la sombra
de la canción que empieza
con la palabra fue.

Song

A piece of bread fallen in clarity
warmed the bed,
the day's underside burns
in countless differences.
That, to know
nothing, to be nothing in the
ocean of lost hands.
Here and there the jumbled
feasts of delirium,
the tree where twilights
linger. Today
tomorrow comes with the day before.
They met on a
journey toward the shadow
of the song that begins
with the word was.

¿Cuánto?

Allí está el aire, el día, la muchacha
que dice pájaros y
nacen pájaros del
nido de su voz, el derrepente
quedado allí nomás. ¿Por qué
levantan compasión en vasitos?
¿Cuánto cobra la herida? ¿Cuánto
le pagan al caballo
que la galopa cada noche?
Arde un espanto que da luz.
Yace
en otro desamparo.

How Much?

There's the wind, the day, the girl
who says birds and
birds are born of
the nest of her voice, the allofasudden
left behind right there. Why
is compassion raised in small glasses?
How much does the wound charge? How much
is the horse paid
for galloping with it each night?
A fear shedding light burns.
It lies
in one more abandoning.

En

¿Dónde? En ésta.
En esta vuelta de su amor
una camisa vina.
Es el raspado de paredes/la
sordera del delirio/¿quién
lo escribe en las venas?/no
da fábulas/calienta
estrechos por donde pasan huecos
sin bandera/las rejas del rapado.
Metieron preso al aire que nacía.
El grillo saca su violín/
recuerda/cuerda.

In

Where? In this one.
In this turning of its love
a shirt wines.
It's the scraping of walls/the
deafness of delirium/who
writes it in their veins?/it
doesn't yield fables/warms
straits where flagless hollows
pass/the railings of the close-cropped.
The air being born was locked up.
The cricket takes out its violin/
records/chords.

Andrea escribe a Marcela

Esa carta de dulzura tan hija
en cielo cae, es la
crecida de repente.
En la prisión de abajo
el mismo amor se calla
cuando lee
esa voz contramuerte.
No sabe más de su deseo redondo.
Pica la piedra del adiós
porque no es cierto.

A Andreíta

Andrea Writes to Marcela

That letter of such daughter sweetness
in heaven falls, it's
suddenly so grown-up.
In the prison below
love itself grows silent
when it reads
that voice againstdeath.
It knows nothing more of its round desire.
It chips away at the farewell stone
because it's not true.

To Andreíta

El encuentro

¿Cómo fue, cómo es todavía?
¿Viste mis ojos en su boca y ella
miró tu silencio o techo
que te abrigaba en Moscú?
¿En la interior de qué celeste
martillaba la roja/qué
gesto de la calle enmudeció cuando
la vida material vio dicha?/¿en
qué hambres pensó tu sudor/dónde
la animalada de la fiebre
tocó tu mujer con después?/
Ahora andan
por púrpuras que el trabajo cansó.
En las preguntas de la madrugada/
padre/te veo montando lenguas
del claro amor/las líneas
de viajes que no contaste
ni a vos mismo.

The Encounter

What was she like, what is she like still?
Did you see my eyes in her mouth and did she
watch your silence or roof
that sheltered you in Moscow?
In the inside of what sky blue
did the red one hammer/what
gesture from the street was struck dumb when
it saw material life spoken?/what
hungers did your sweat think of/where
did the fever's beastliness
touch your wife with after?/
Now they move
through purples tired by work.
In the early morning questions/
father/I see you riding tongues
of clear love/travel
lines you didn't even tell
yourself.

Amparos

El aire, la roca, el péndulo, la
claridad de la noche
dan noticias del mundo que
nadie sabe leer. ¿Son ellas
para ellas, no más? Las sábanas
arrugadas del día
envuelven un fulgor cercado
por rostros que se acaban.
Su solo amparo es el
delirio del deseo.

Shelters

The air, the rock, the pendulum, the
clarity of the night
give news of the world
no one knows how to read. Are they
for them, nothing more? The day's
rumpled sheets
wrap up a flash fenced in
by used up faces.
Their only shelter is the
delirium of desire.

Avenidas

Cuando pasan a la
distancia por un colador
quedan muchos pájaros
en el colador. Pájaros de
ida y de vuelta, pensamientos
que no se quieren acostar.
Es el otro por uno
con su viaje de tiempo. Hay
parajes del origen, ríos, casas.
Las avenidas de la búsqueda
cesan en ellas mismas,
lo no encontrado canta
sin terminar. Los pájaros
cambian de vida
y preguntan lo mismo siempre.

Avenues

When they pass in the
distance through a sieve
many birds stay
in the sieve. Birds
coming and going, thoughts
unwilling to lie down.
It's the other for one
with its journey of time. There are
lands of origin, rivers, houses.
The avenues of the search
cease in themselves,
the unfound sings
endlessly. The birds
change their lives
and ask the same as always.

Pisadas

Aydiós qué sueño, dijo
el gran espantapájaros que espanta
verdades del perdido. La
suave pampa de ayer
donde trotaban las mañanas
que ya no cantan y
las brisas habladoras hoy
en las conjugaciones de la muerte.
Manos deshechas en la mano
de la memoria y su tamaño triste.
Las dádivas de la frontera
donde la voz y su exterior se encuentran
en las bodas de la
pisada del caballo y el caballo.
Eso que es máscara en
los dos pedazos de la lengua.

Hoofprints

Ohgod I'm sleepy, said
the great scarecrow who scares
the lost one's truths. The
soft pampas of yesterday
where the mornings
that no longer sing trotted and
today the talkative breezes
in the conjugations of death.
Hands undone in the hand
of memory and its sad size.
The gifts of the border
where the voice and its outside meet up
at the wedding of the
horse's hoofprint and the horse.
What is a mask in
the tongue's two pieces.

Malena

La Malena que sale de la voz
oscura, dura, seca,
deja espectros en medio de la calle.
Odia como hay que odiar, con grande amor,
hace cuerpo en la boca.
Lo que le come le es devuelto,
cambia sus alhajas heladas
en piedra que arde.
Vuelve a Malena
la luz que en soledad vivía.

Malena

The Malena emerging from the
dark, hard, dry voice
leaves spectrums behind in the middle of the
    street.
She hates like you have to hate, with a great love,
she forms a body in her mouth.
What eats her is brought back up,
changes her frozen jewels
into burning stone.
To Malena returns
the light once living in solitude.

Es

el caballo escondido que
crece en el viento/
es amor/la cuchara
que revolvió antifaces y

cambió la sopa de la vida/es
amor/los jinetes de la noche
que galopan silbando son
amor/la palabra de las

constelaciones y el animalito
que las pasea/amor/y amor
es la niña que despierta la calle

con su manita llena de
caricias/contra
la nada limpia/

Is

the hidden horse
rising in the wind/
is love/the spoon
that stirred masks and

changed the soup of life/is
love/the night riders
galloping and whistling are
love/the word of the

constellations and the tiny animal
that takes them for a walk/love/and love
is the girl who awakens the street

with her tiny hand full of
caresses/against
the clean nothingness/

Tango

El tango que dice hay dolor
que no se cura con lágrimas
vigila un sueño.
En el cielo del tiempo donde
domeñan las tormentas
con fragancia furiosa
vive un trazo de sangre que
la infamia dejó en el camino.
Hay que hacer un paquete con sol,
con los miembros del sol.

Tango

The tango that says there's ache
tears can't cure
watches over a dream.
In the sky of time where
storms tame
with a furious fragrance
lives a stroke of blood
left on the path by infamy.
You've got to make a bundle with sun,
with the limbs of the sun.

Foto

la foto del poeta/ciega/
no da la luz con la que vio
los cauces del amor/dorados
por el odio/las causas
que no abren la boca/la
grande cosa de la pasión inútil/
o mundo donde hubiéramos/canta
el sueño del horror/las escondidas
visiones más allá/
el destello de la palabra única/
su silencio de abajo/
el jacaranda que palpita/

A *Rubén Bonifaz Nuño*

Photo

the photo of the poet/blinds/
doesn't shed the light he saw
the courses of love with/gilded
by hate/the causes
that won't open their mouths/the
great thing of useless passion/
or world where we would have/sings
the dream of horror/the hidden
visions beyond/
the wake of the lone word/
its silence from below/
the jacaranda quivering/

To Rubén Bonifaz Nuño

Andrea

Danza, danza y encuentra
verdad en el error, ansias que
huelen a leche madre.
El soplo de los astros
la viste de
la blanca luz en el recinto
donde la vida crece
en las manitas de su vez.
Está llena de bienes
que en lo más hondo de su pie
pisan desastres y desgracias.
Nadie conoce el nombre
del páis que existe
entre su corazón y las
ramas del humo.

Andrea

Dances, dances and finds
truth in the error, anguishes
smelling of mother milk.
The astral blowing
dresses her in
the white light in the enclosure
where life grows
in the tiny hands of her turn.
She's full of goods
that in the deepest part of her foot
trample on disasters and disgraces.
No one knows the name
of the country that exists
between her heart and the
smoke branches.

Volver

El pasado vuelve cuando
desaparece. Vacíos que lloran
en sus países
y en arrabales interiores gritan.
¿Qué vale la cerviz golpeada mucho?
Oh cuerpos que navegan
la sangre todavía y en
el viejo amor se juntan.
El miedo en rostros ya tocados
es piedra que repite su piedra.
Se hinchan los ojos con
las cobardías de este tiempo,
sentadas
en sillas de su olvido.

A Marco Antonio Campos

To Return

The past returns when
it disappears. Voids crying
in their countries
and shouting out in inner slums.
What's the badly beaten nape worth?
Oh bodies that still sail
over blood and in
old love come together.
The fear in faces once touched
is stone repeating its stone.
The eyes swell with
the cowardices of this time,
sitting
on seats of its oblivion.

To Marco Antonio Campos

Pedazos

En los pespuntes del amor
hay un odio cosido a la ventura.
¿Por qué? pregunta la pequeña y
tiembla en el bosque de la vida.
La calabaza se
ha perdido en el cuento incinerado.
Cortan al niño
que anda de botas altas y entra
agua limpia en el alma.
Con sus pedazos hacen
bombas, cañones, infelices.

Pieces

In love's backstitches
there's a hate sewn to happiness.
Why? asks the little girl and
she trembles in the forest of life.
The pumpkin's
gotten lost in the incinerated story.
Someone's chopped up the boy
who walks around in tall boots and
clean water enters the soul.
With his pieces they make
bombs, cannons, the wretched.

Alrededor

Oiga, maestro, luispedrojoaquín,
usted, ¿quién es? ¿Por qué
se parece a mis perros de invierno,
nada que los detenga
en morder mi destino? Eso
me pregunta quién soy
entre cantos desnudos.
La mancha dividida del alba
me pregunta quién fui.
¿Acaso fui? El otoño
cubre de hojas la
espléndida pregunta. Salgo
sin rimas de papel
bajo los vuelos de la lluvia.
Entre yo y yo hay
interrupciones y
miro al otro de mí como un ladrón
que se roba a sí mismo.
Un gato cruza
la calle entre los dos.

Around

Excuse me, maestro, luispedrojoaquin,
who are you? Why
do you look like my winter dogs,
nothing to stop them
from biting my destiny? All that
asks me who I am
among naked cantos.
The divided dawn stain
asks me who I was.
Was I actually? Autumn
covers the splendid
question with leaves. I part
with no paper rhymes
beneath the flights of rain.
Between me and me there are
interruptions and
I watch the other of me like a thief
stealing from himself.
A cat crosses
the street between the two.

Baires

la barriada/al crepúsculo/finge
recuerdos que
se detienen en un momento de oro/
tango que fue en los pies de la
muchacha más linda del salón/
la de pechos que hablaban/parecía
la muerte/que nunca iba a llegar/
sueños/granos de polvo/
en perdederas del adiós/crepúsculo/
roto ahora en la boca
de la ciudad que existe/
en una caricia vieja/

Baires

the neighborhood/at twilight/fakes
memories that
linger in a golden moment/
tango once in the feet of the
most beautiful girl in the room/
the one with breasts that spoke/she looked
like the death/that would never arrive/
dreams/grains of dust/
in wastings of farewell/twilight/
broken now in the mouth
of the city existing/
in an old caress/

Gorri

El fuego de tu mano
queda en el mundo, quema
suciedades terrestres,
llena la copa de buen ojo,
el que mira oleajes
de amor y de dolor, ese fuego
funda ciudades, soles
que no se ven, para a
los mazos que golpean
en pabellones del espanto, piedra es
contra la perra de la injuria,
las mañanas sin leche, las
llagas del corazón,
el fuego de tu mano arde
dentrísimo de vos, desde vos,
empeñado en alzar
lo que es y no fue,
mares/ mareas/vida/siempre/

Gorri

The fire of your hand
lingers in the world, chars
earthly dirtiness,
fills the cup with good eye,
the one watching swells
of love and ache, that fire
founds cities, suns
that can't see each other, stops
the mallets from hammering
in pavilions of fear, stone is
against the bitch of slander,
the milkless mornings, the
heart's sores,
the fire of your hand burns
so very within you, from you,
determined to raise
what is and wasn't,
seas/sea tides/life/always/

La pretensión

El disparate de la tristeza y
sus animales que
hurgan por todos lados
son más verdaderos que yo.
Estas palabras
son más verdaderas que yo.
Son materia y no tiempo,
en sus entrañas hay
una piedra que nunca se acaba.
Los hijos de los hombres creen
que mojarlas con vino
les quitará conciencia, fuego.
Hay palabras que esperan y nadie las toma.
Solas ahí en silencio florido.

The Aspiration

The nonsense of sadness and
its animals
rummaging everywhere
are truer than I.
These words
are truer than I.
They are matter and not time,
in their insides there's
a never-ending stone.
The children of men think
wetting them with wine
will get rid of some consciousness, fire.
There are words waiting and no one takes them.
On their own there in flowering silence.

El estornino

averaver/locura/cámbiese
en estornino de verano/hay/
desiertos que preguntan cómo
la suerte huye del humano.
Bajo el puente de piedra/
cómplices sin querer
hierven en sangre cada día/
escriben ay en la libreta
de la frente de adentro/se arrancan
fiebres en un rincón.
Estornino de cielo hinchado
por disimulos/
furias que no se van/
caballo fijo/
en una pampa ciega.

The Starling

let'sseelet'ssee/madness/change
to a summer starling/there are/
deserts asking how
luck flees from the human.
Beneath the stone bridge/
unintentional accomplices
boil in blood each day/
write oh in the notebook
of the inside forehead/uproot
fevers in a corner.
Starling of a sky swelled
by slynesses/
furies that won't go away/
fixed horse/
on a blind pampa.

Lecturas

La niña lee
el alfabeto de los árboles
y se vuelve ave clara. Cuánta
paciencia ha de tener en aulas
donde le enseñan a no ser.
El temblor atascado
en su garganta es mudo.
También es mundo que
acosan los que saben. Así aprende
a montar monstruos de ojos pérfidos
y cuando vuelve a la que fue
ve el tiempo lastimado.

Readings

The little girl reads
the tree alphabet
and turns into a clear bird. So much
patience she must have in classrooms
where they teach her not to be.
The tremble wedged
in her throat is wordless.
It's also world
harassed by those who know. So she learns
to mount monsters with treacherous eyes
and when she turns back into what she was
she sees time wounded.

Azares

El compañero ata
sus alas al azar, lava los platos
del día, la cuchara le da
palazos de memoria cuando
servía sopas que vendrán, es tarde
y es temprano el llanto que
moja el tiempo que se quedó en un tiempo,
pensando en su volver.
El compañero lava
crepitaciones verdes en la mano
que lava y
su ya no está disuelve
bestias del odio, canta
bajito y tanto en un rincón.

Fates

The comrade weds
his wings to fate, washes the day's
dishes, the spoon wallops him
with shovel blows of memory when
he served soups to come, it's late
and it's soon the cry
wetting the time that lingered in a time,
thinking about its return.
The comrade washes
green crepitations in the hand
washing and
his no longer here dissolves
beasts of hate, sings
real low and so much in a corner.

Las águilas

Las águilas que piden la bebida
asomada al adiós
no están borrachas, hacen
caminos hacia
todo lo que no es vida. Con
ejércitos de trago piden
fortalezas del ánimo que un ciego
no puede construir. Las pieles del
olvido se secaron
un verano cualquiera, sostenían
tactos de la memoria en su violenta
contracción y empujaban
el atrás hacia atrás.
Con tanta sangre, digo.

The Eagles

The eagles that ask for the drink
peeping out of the farewell
aren't drunk, they forge
paths toward
everything that's not life. With
armies of drink they ask for
fortresses of spirit a blind man
can't build. The skins of
oblivion dried
on any given summer, held
the touches of memory in its violent
contraction and pushed
the back backward.
With so much blood, I mean.

Piojos

Si el ritmo de un poema
trae vino y mece
las sombras y mamá,
quitame los piojos que traje de la escuela,
papá,
no saques tu cinturón contra mí:
eso que sopla en una esquina
es mi querer de vos, es un
niño en la calle
sin comprender. ¿Qué hacés ahí
envuelto en odios
que nunca pude resolver?
¿Qué castigabas cuando me
castigabas?
No te pregunto, me pregunto.
Ya sé que es tarde para todo, menos
este saber de vos que no se sabe.
Te quisiera a mi lado
en el silencio que me diste
y calla como un buey.

Lice

If the rhythm of a poem
brings wine and sways
the shadows and mama,
pick out the lice I brought home from school,
papa,
don't take your belt off against me:
what's blowing in a corner
is my love for you, it's a
boy on the street
not understanding. What are you doing there
wrapped in hates
I could never settle?
What did you punish when
you punished me?
I'm not asking you, it's me I'm asking.
I know it's too late for everything now save
this knowing of you unknown.
I'd like you at my side
in the silence you granted me
and it quiets like an ox.

Plato

A ver, mi plato, en qué te lavo
esta noche que vienen
los cántaros del tiempo
con mi pensar pesar. Llevate
compañeros bebidos
en tanta copa que
no los trae de vuelta. Mirar hondo
en los copos de ausencia que se funden
al sol es la miseria, nombres
de aquí y de allá donde estuvieran.
Llamá amor al reverso
de estas heridas, mucho.
Plato donde comí
sobras.

Plate

Let's see, my plate, where should I wash you
tonight when cruses
of time come
with my tribulation thinking. Take away
comrades drunk
in so much cup that
it doesn't bring them back. To look deep
into the flakes of absence melting
in the sun is misery, names
from here and there wherever they were.
Call love on the reverse
of these wounds, a lot.
Plate where I ate
leftovers.

La camisa

La luz que toca mi camisa
nada sabe de mí. La recibo,
pero quién la merece.
Poner el cielo al fuego es una
condición de este tiempo, el almanaque
finge inocencia en su papel.
Los bárbaros que manejan las penas
de los demás, espinan
astros que no vendrán.
¿Qué esperan los dolidos en su cueva
con una cama donde
espantos, miedos, duermen cada noche?
El no mundo conversa
con mañanas sin Dios.

The Shirt

The light grazing my shirt
knows nothing of me. I welcome it,
but who deserves it.
To place the sky on the fire is a
condition of these times, the almanac
fakes innocence on its paper.
The barbarians who manage the sorrows
of others, they puncture
the astral unwilling to come.
What do the wounded await in their cave
with a bed where
fears, frights, sleep each night?
The no world converses
with Godless mornings.

Otoñar

Hay que hacerlo con gran
respeto por las hojas. Su amarillo
es un resto de sol y dice
que el alma es un
ejercicio del alma. Si no,
se le va el techo y las tormentas
embarran el lenguaje. De ahí
no nacen hombre ni mujer, apenas
espejos de las grietas
sin luz lunar ni humo
que esconda puertas mal cerradas.
Lo que se oxida es el recuerdo
de uno mismo
en vociferaciones de la frase.
Alguien riega los astros
y la madera crece.

To Autumn

You've got to do it with a great
respect for the leaves. Their yellow
is a residue of sun and says
the soul is an
exercise of the soul. If not,
its roof blows away and the storms
muddy language. From there
no man or woman is born, just
mirrors of the crevices
with no lunar light or smoke
hiding poorly shut doors.
What rusts is the memory
of yourself
in vociferations of the phrase.
Someone waters the astral
and the wood grows.

Habilidades

El otoño se decolora, triste,
cuando poetas hábiles
en la abyección, pisan la
poesía, su fuego,
por un puestito. Ese
crimen les cuesta vida, no
se queman en el
pulso de su voz única
y nada alcanzan a nombrar.
Triste, triste, es la cara
del manco o ciego que
deja el vacío por la nada.
El apagamiento de su música
grazna en libros torcidos.

A Marco Antonio Campos

Skills

Autumn becomes discolored, sad,
when poets skillful
in abjection trample
poetry, its fire,
for some small post. That
crime costs them life, they
don't burn in the
pulse of their unique voices
and manage to name nothing.
Sad, sad, are the faces
of the one-armed or blind who
leave the void for nothingness.
The fading away of their music
caws in twisted books.

To Marco Antonio Campos

La diosa

La diosa Palabra, o búfala, o leona,
sólo visita a los que ama.
Ahí desviste su imposible belleza
que no se puede tocar. Fugaz
y siempre huyendo, no
roza la mano de nadie, come
de su silencio y entra
en abismos donde
pasa en una carreta el adiós.
Ah, diosa que así mostrás la muerte
a tu esposo perpetuo.
Saben los que te roban
que crujís triste.

The Goddess

The goddess Word, or bisoness, or lioness,
only visits those she loves.
There she undresses her impossible beauty
that can't be touched. Fleeting
and always fleeing, she
brushes no one's hand, eats
from her silence and enters
abysses where
farewell passes by on a wagon.
Oh, goddess you show death like so
to your perpetual spouse.
Those who steal you away know
you crackle sadly.

Problemas

En mí ordeno tu amor,
acosado de sueños sueño
en limpideces que un fantasma ensucia.
¿Tendrá la lámpara más luz y cuándo
los recados del mundo
no serán yo? Quietísismas
las aves del consuelo, aquí no vuelan.
En su sombra
alguna vez viví. El disfraz
de árbol del árbol no
está libre
de las molestias del pasado.
La vida involuntaria alza
su animalejo trunco.

Problems

In me I put your love in order,
hounded by dreams I dream
of clean things dirtied by a ghost.
Might the lamp shed more light and when
will the world's messages
not be me? So very still
the birds of solace, they don't fly here.
In their shadow
I once lived. The tree's
tree disguise
isn't free
from the troubles of the past.
The involuntary life raises
its vermin cut short.

Espasmos

quien escucha la noche/los
espasmos que hierven y
saquean las terrazas/jacintos
que se detienen
en calles donde había nombres/casas
de no dormir/las obras
como pasión de vida
que iba a la muerte/en ese perro
caben las pieles de la historia
no escritas todavía/o sólo
en rostros que se fueron
con el deseo bajo el brazo/

Spasms

whoever listens to the night/the
spasms boiling and
plundering the terraces/hyacinths
lingering
on streets where there were names/homes
not for sleeping/the works
like passion of life
once going toward death/in that dog
fit the skins of history
still to be written/or only
on faces that left
with desire under their arms/

El puñal

El puñal marroquí
conoció sangre humana. Ahora
el olvido le come
la hoja que brillaba al sol.
Calla en su vaina y nada
le quita el gran desierto,
los caballos. ¿Qué hacés, eternidad,
en este humilde acero, es
tu condición raspada por
las furias del metal? ¿Los párpados
que cerraba la herida? ¿Brumas
con madre alrededor?

A Marco Antonio Campos

The Dagger

The Moroccan dagger
knew human blood. Now
oblivion eats
its leaf that glistened in the sun.
It falls silent in its sheath and nothing
can clear away the great desert,
the horses. What are you doing, eternity,
in this humble steel, is
your condition grazed by
the metal furies? The eyelids
closed by the wound? Mists
with mother all around?

To Marco Antonio Campos

La cama

En la cama semidesierta yace
tu aroma azul. Mis manos
tropiezan con
el vacío/tu rostro.

The Bed

In the semideserted bed lies
your azure aroma. My hands
stumble over
the void/your face.

Nacer nacer

Abren las puertas del arrabal. Allí
la palabra canora cuenta
el tiempo que no pasó. Perdemos
la calle que se derrite en
el chapaleo de la vida breve
al sol de la verdad.
¡Espléndida cosecha de
almas desordenadas que no saben
por qué está gris el pulso/triste
la pasión que encendía
sus ángeles de guerra
y hoy no puede venir! ¡Y suben
libros del corazón que el deseo
tapó de luz!

To Be Born To Be Born

The doors of the slum open. There
the tuneful word tells of
the time not passing. We lose
the street melting in
the splash of the brief life
under the sun of truth.
Splendid harvest of
jumbled souls who don't know
why the pulse is gray/sad
the passion that ignited
its angels of war
and cannot come today! And they rise,
the books of the heart desire
covered in light!

Está

Caliente está el envés
de lo luchado/el gran
sueño como animal
sobre el pulmón que lo respira.
Un alfiler en la garganta lee
palabras que no salen. Afuera
crecen los granos repartidos
de la desdicha. ¿Quién empuja
a las bestias que comen en la mesa
con nosotros mismitos?
Se sientan
sin saludar, tapan el sol.

Is

Hot is the underside
of the struggled/the great
dream like an animal
over the lung breathing it.
A pin in the throat reads
words not appearing. Outside
grow the scattered grains
of unhappiness. Who pushes
the beasts that eat at the table
with little old us?
They sit
not greeting, they block the sun.

Envolturas

Vos, que envolvés
el tibio aroma y la espiral de la
noche indormida en
las vendas del cobarde y
fingís que sos sin ser vivido:
¡abrite las mil puertas
de tu ciudad cerrada! En el rincón
donde el miedo te agachó la cabeza
hay esperas que dicen
abur abur. Te fuiste, no dejaste
que una luz te sacara
de vos a la luz de tu luz.
Caen estrellas y está triste
Dios, que existe poquito.

Wrappings

You, who wraps
the warm aroma and the spiral of the
unslept night in
the coward's bandages and
fakes that you are without being lived:
open the thousand doors
of your closed city! In the corner
where fear lowered your head
there are waits saying
so long so long. You left, you didn't let
one light take you out
of you in the light of your light.
Stars fall and sad is
God, who exists just a little.

Par impar

La música del verso
debe ser impar, decía Verlaine
en un París desolado por la
falta de amor a Verlaine.
La soledad es madre
contraria al octosílabo
y al decasílabo, compadres.
Debieran saber eso, ustedes tan
solos frente a ustedes
en un papel lleno de
imposibilidad.
En ese estado, el alma
no rima con el ritmo
del corazón. Está absorta
en vibraciones del vacío. Un gato
se ofrece a ser poema.

Even Odd

The music of verse
should be odd, said Verlaine
in a Paris pillaged by the
lack of love for Verlaine.
Solitude is a mother
opposed to octosyllable
and decasyllable, compadres.
You ought to know that, all of you so
alone facing all of you
on a sheet of paper filled with
impossibility.
In that state, the soul
doesn't rhyme with the rhythm
of the heart. It's soaked up
in the void's vibrations. A cat
offers to be a poem.

Pelícanos

Allí está el potro
en aguas del entendimiento, la
nube que borra
espejos del lenguaje. Dura
la incomprensión de los pelícanos
sin techo, ellos, bellos
aliados del
río del corazón. El día abrasa
los hilos y las formas
de las aguas sin cuerpo. Cae
una muralla momentánea
sobre la colina amarilla
donde la boca de la noche
besa.

Pelicans

There's the colt
in waters of understanding, the
cloud that erases
mirrors of language. What lasts is
the incomprehension of pelicans
roofless, they, lovely
allies of
the heart's river. The day scorches
the threads and the shapes
of bodiless waters. A
momentous wall falls
over the yellow hill
where the mouth of the night
kisses.

¿Qué se sabe?

Del poema, nada. Llega, tiembla
y raspa un fósforo apagado.
¿Se le ve algo? Nada. Tiende una
mano para aferrar
las olitas de tiempo que pasan
por la voz de un jilguero. ¿Qué
agarró? Nada. La
ave se fue a lo no sonado
en un cuarto que gira sin
recordación ni espérames.
Hay muchos nombres en la lluvia.
¿Qué sabe el poema? Nada.

What Do You Know?

Of the poem, nothing. It arrives, trembles
and strikes a match snuffed out.
Can you see something of it? Nothing. It offers a
hand to catch hold of
the tiny waves of time flowing
through the voice of a saffron finch. What
did it catch hold of? Nothing. The
bird went to the unsounded
in a room spinning with no
recollection or waitformes.
There're so many names in the rain.
What does the poem know? Nothing.

Distribuciones

Si el dolor es físico y de alma
el sufrimiento, díganme
cómo se distribuye la pasión
del cuerpalma, sus bestias
volátiles, distintas
de la eternidad. ¿Se separan
cuando los números profundos
dijeron basta y lo
que calentaba el corazón se fue?
En la mitad del ser un incendio
aterido y sin luz
saca un pañuelo y limpia
pueblos de la conciencia.

A José Ángel Leyva

Distributions

If ache is physical and suffering of
the soul, tell me
how the passion
of the bodysoul is distributed, its volatile
beasts, different
from eternity. Do they separate
when the deep numbers
said that's enough and what
heated the heart left?
In the middle of being a fire
freezing and lightless
takes out a kerchief and cleans
peoples of their consciousness.

To José Angel Leyva

Interrupciones

¿qué se pierde en el salto?/¿los
otoños del pasado/el ansia
de haber vivido no/la des-
esperación de cartas que no llegan?/
¿únicos nombres de la noche?/
¿por qué el ángel que vuela
hacia adelante mira atrás?/furia
que interrumpís/ya vámonos/
poema, vámonos/¿a dónde
se fue el ombú que te crecía
y
contaba cosas de la lluvia?
¿a dónde irán palabras que
no pudieron nacer/y
venían en barco como
demostraciones de un mar corto?/
¿en que vacío entraron/puras/
pegadas a mis muertos?

Interruptions

what get's lost in the jump?/the
autumns of the past/the anxiety
of having lived not/the des-
peration of letters that don't arrive?/
lone names of the night?/
why does the angel flying
forward look back?/fury
you interrupt/let's go now/
poem, let's go/where
did the ombu tree go that grew on you and
told things of the rain?/
where will the words go that
couldn't be born/and
came on a ship like
displays of a short sea?
in which void did they enter/pure/
clinging to my dead?

Velocidades

del calor al frío/con la
velocidad de la miseria/pasan
lenguas con escorpiones/almas
secas por la
ausencia de alma/en lo más alto de
su balbucear flamea
la soledad de gris vestida/
muertos caminan por la calle/fingen
que son/fabrican
despiertes en la madrugada/tienen
el cuello reclinado sobre
las maldades flamantes/

Velocities

from heat to cold/with the
velocity of wretchedness/tongues
pass by with scorpions/souls
dried by the
absence of soul/at the heights of
their babble blazes
solitude dressed in gray/
dead walk down the street/fake
being/fashion
wakeups in early morning/lean
their necks back on
the shiny evils/

La muchacha

Algo amenaza a la muchacha
cuando ella se visita el amor.
Cataratas de frío/
viento que duele como piedra/
lejanías de la alta vida/los
planetas que empuja la cuchara
y giran mudos en la sopa.
Sube la noche/toca
su lucecita dulce/encorva
las espaldas para que no se apague.
En otro perfecto mundo/ella/
danza, y el color. Cuánto de sueño/
mucho/desplomado
en sábanas solísimas.

The Girl

Something threatens the girl
when she visits her love.
Cascades of cold/
wind hurts like stone/
distances of the steep life/the
planets pushed by the spoon
and spinning mute in the soup.
Night rises/touches
her sweet little light/curves
her back so it won't go out.
In another perfect world/she/
dances, and the color. How much dream/
plenty/collapsed
on sheets so solitary.

La foto

A las cuatro de la tarde de marzo
en una vieja foto
las rosas se volvieron a abrir.
La vida no apagó
su aroma ni
la brisa que pasaba lenta
con fechas del paisaje. Una
muñeca es todavía en
la manita que toca el universo,
tibia. Alrededor
se ve un vuelo de pájaros idos.
Al fondo,
el ser que es haber sido lee
lo que el tiempo escribió.

A Paola

The Photo

At four in the March afternoon
the roses flowered again
in an old photo.
Life didn't snuff out
their aroma nor
did the breeze slowly passing by
with landscape dates. A
doll is still in
the tiny hand that touches the universe,
warm. All around
you see a flight of birds gone.
In the background,
the being who is to have been reads
what time wrote.

To Paola

Ecco

objetos/cosas/la mesada/
mapas/sombreros/el volcán
dormido/sillas donde
se sienta mi acabar/el día/
lo furioso/lo angélico del día/
hojas que caen/callejones/
rigodones/tornillos/los ojazos
de una guitarra ciega/juntamente
pedazos del mío ser/escándalos
del muro/llaves/la
historia hecha de seda/voces/carros/
pancartas de la muerte/oh/
declive de los fuegos/la
camisa amarga/astros/el mantel/
lecciones del relámpago/la hueca
sombra de boca para adentro/
postes/zapatos/máquinas/
el temblor blanco de Teresa en
tierraguas del tormento ancho/
las comas/la escalera/el fin
del náufrago
universal idéntico/los mares
que tragan tardes que iban/el hotel
demasiado preciso/golpes
sordos/tapias/lo barrio/pies
lejos de mí/tan solos/platos/
la sopa de mamá/nubes que
forman ojos perdidos/labios
que besan lo que fue/todo eso/todo/
y más que los compases del
universo que enumera el tiempo
estás ahí/poesía/
¿te hallarás/
hundida en este mundo?/
¿bella vos que bellás/
hundida en este mundo?

Ecco

objects/things/monthly wages/
maps/hats/the sleeping
volcano/seats where
my beover sits/the day/
the furious/the angelic of the day/
falling leaves/alleyways/
rigaudons/screws/the big eyes
of a blind guitar/jointly
pieces of mine being/scandals
of the wall/keys/the
history made of silk/voices/cars/
death banners/oh/
fire decline/the
bitter shirt/astral/the tablecloth/
lightning lessons/the hollow
shadow not paid service by lips/
posts/shoes/machines/
Teresa's white tremble in
terrawaters of wide torment/
the commas/the stairstep/the end
of the shipwreck
universal identical/the seas
swallowing evenings that went/the hotel
excessively precise/deaf
blows/barriers/what's neighborhood/feet
far from me/so alone/plates/
mama's soup/clouds giving
shape to lost eyes/lips
kissing what was/all that/all/
and more than the rhythms of the
universe tallying time
you're there/poetry/
will you find yourself/
sunken in this world?/
beautiful you beautifulling/
sunken in this world?

Caminos

Mujeres, hombres, niños, díganme.
La niebla no ha salido
y el aire arropa el pabellón
de los solos. Un otoño arrugado
le da la mano a pérdidas, los sastres
no las saben coser. En el camino
cae lo ciego del andar, palabras
arrancadas al cuerpo, los pedazos
de una ausencia que cruje.
Las fábricas del frío no
pueden tapar la boca
abierta a vientos de nacer
en los kilómetros de insomnio
a caminar todavía.

Paths

Women, men, children, tell me.
The mist hasn't left
and the air dresses the ward
of the lonely. A wrinkled autumn
lends a hand for losses, the tailors
don't know how to sew them. On the path
falls the blind from going about, words
torn from the body, the pieces
of a creaking absence.
Frost's factories can't
cover the mouth
open to winds of birth
in the kilometers of sleeplessness
still to walk.

Nieblas

Aparecen con niebla
los rostros muertos hacia arriba y
compañeros que no se oyen
miran el mundo.
El río abre las piernas
de una mujer y pasa
la delgadez de abril. País
de la desdicha
que no se va, no anda
enamorado de
la que canta en un lecho florido.
Poesía,
atás la sombra a su vértigo/
a la fatalidad a su respiro/
vuelo que
no conoce el perdón.

Mists

They appear with mist
the faces dead upward and
comrades who can't hear each another
watch the world.
The river opens the legs
of a woman and
the thinness of April flows. Country
of the unhappiness
that won't go away, it doesn't go around
in love with
the one singing in a flowered bed.
Poetry,
you bind shadow to its vertigo/
fatality to its breath/
flight
unknowing of pardon.

Reflexiones

Con miedo de lo que iba a venir,
con miedo de lo que iba a pasar
hoy, mañana, una aguja clavada
en la mitad, ahí,
¿la esfinge de uno mismo?
No músicas angélicas,
no la gracia de la flauta con
una luna en la lengua, no
sílabas de la frente que deja
caer cantares de la esposa/
abierta/su candor
que vive en todas las cucharas.
Los lindes de la tierra cocida
en los lugares donde el otro
cada noche estaciona y sufre.
¿Últimos tratos con espejos
donde me vi posterior? ¿Luz
sin cielo/sangre que
no sirve para nada? ¿El otro
sin mí? ¿Morí por él sin mí?
Las llaves de la casa
nunca tuvieron casa.

A Lucila Pagliai

Reflections

Scared of what was coming,
scared of what was going to happen
today, tomorrow, a needle stuck
in the middle, there,
the sphinx of one's self?
No angelic music,
no flute grace with
a moon on the tongue, no
syllables from the forehead that lets
fall the songs of the spouse/
open/her candor
living in all the spoons.
The limits of the earth stewed
in the places where the other
parks and suffers each night.
Last dealings with mirrors
where I saw myself posterior? Light
minus sky/blood that's
completely useless? The other
minus me? Did I die for him minus me?
The house keys
never had a house.

To Lucila Pagliai

Novedades

Sueño mi sueño preferido
y la noche no termina nunca.
Los árboles muestran su alfabeto
y astros que
hablan del infinito
de cada soplo del vivir.
Construyo madres idas
con la mano puesta en la noche.
¡Qué bello era su rincón
donde ecos vagos la nombraban!
Así, de espaldas a mí,
se fugaba a un país besado
por su aterida juventud.
Madre que
cocinabas distancias
en las ollas del día.
Todavía me hablás
en las grietas del tiempo.

Novelties

I dream my favorite dream
and the night never ends.
The trees show their alphabet
and astral
that speak of the infinite
in each gust of living.
I build mothers gone
with my hand placed on the night.
How beautiful her corner was
where vague echoes named her!
Like so, with her back to me,
she would flee to a country kissed
by her youth stiff with cold.
Mother who
stewed distances
in the day's pots.
You still talk to me
in the crevices of time.

Espera

Te adelantaste mucho, furia,
con tu collar de hielo. Espérame,
voy a entrar en tu casa.
Comés traiciones,
el amargo sabor de los arrepentidos.
Nadie sabe qué hicieron con
su pasado, allí iban tristes
de mundo, pensaban
que eran el otro con dolor.
Ahora su culpa es odio.
Dejan caer pedazos de
un veneno sin gracia.

Wait

You're far ahead, fury,
with your icy collar. Wait for me,
I'm going to enter your house.
You eat betrayals,
the bitter savor of the repented.
No one knows what they did to
their past, there they walked around sad
from world, thought
they were the other aching.
Now their guilt is hate.
They let fall pieces of
a graceless poison.

Juegos

La baraja que ignora su destino
lanza una voz muda y se enfría
en las lecciones del azar.
Alza el vuelo a la pregunta del
ni acá, ni allá, ni dónde.
Entre palabras hay
ese tejido o casamiento
del sí y del no, la grande
condición de la llama
que arde donde quiere.
El sentimiento busca
una apariencia de color.
Persigue nombres
que no se dejan nombrar.

Games

The deck of cards disregarding its destiny
launches a mute voice and grows cold
in the lessons of chance.
It takes flight to the question not from
here, or there, or wherever.
Among words there's
that weaving or marriage
of yes and no, the great
condition of the flame
burning wherever it wants.
Feeling searches for
an appearance of color.
It shadows names
that refuse to be named.

Pérdidas

Se me perdió una palabra que
acompañaba "universal". ¿Hay alguna
que pueda acompañar "universal"?
¿La paz "universal"?
¿El amor "universal"?
¿El universo es "universal"?
Cuántas comillas para
decir que el mundo existe.
Los astros
no están de fiesta, Mallarmé,
y no hay midinette o
costurerita que nos salve.

Losses

I lost a word that
went with "universal." Is there one
that goes with "universal"?
"Universal" peace?
"Universal" love?
Is the universe "universal"?
So many quotation marks to
say the world exists.
The astral
isn't festive, Mallarmé,
and there's no midinette or
tiny seamstress to save us.

Callar

Una ola de amor que
va de mi cuerpo al tuyo es
una humana canción.
No canta, vuela entre
tu boca y mi verano
bajo tu sol. El calendario no
tiene esta noche o fecha en su papel.
El manantial de vos
cae como vino en la copa
y el mundo calla sus desastres.
Gracias, mundo, por no ser más que mundo
y ninguna otra cosa.

A Mara

To Silence

A wave of love
flowing from my body to yours is
a human song.
It doesn't sing, it flies between
your mouth and my summer
beneath your sun. The calendar doesn't
have tonight or this date on its paper.
The spring of you
falls like wine in the glass
and the world silences its disasters.
Thank you, world, for not being more than world
and nothing else.

To Mara

A saber

El dolor da poco de comer
y siempre da lo mismo.
Oscuro, oscuro,
cada vez más oscuro
el plato repetido, la ruindad
que abre los brazos para recibir.
Trastos que alteran la casa con
cenizas del que ardió.
¿No amaba?
¿No le dolía el mundo,
el sol mal repartido?
Hay miserables que olvidan
lo que viajaron de sí al otro.
Sus babas no apagan el tiempo con
charletas que dicen amén.

To Wit

The ache doesn't nourish much
and it always nourishes the same.
Dark, dark,
darker and darker
the repeating plate, the meanness
opening its arms to receive.
Junk altering the house with
ashes of one burned.
Didn't he love?
Didn't his world ache,
his poorly distributed sun?
There are wicked people who forget
what they traveled from themselves to the other.
Their drool doesn't douse time with
chatterers who say amen.

Exposiciones

Raro el que se muestra
a sí mismo a sí mismo, los
espejos mienten, se sabe, y la madera
del cajón a la vista
no arregla nada.
El ojo de la eternidad ajado
vuelve bella a la luna
y la sangre aquí abajo
parece plata. De plata
es el sueño invencible, el deseo
que las balas no pueden matar.
Mañana es otro día dice
el día que pasó.
No estoy en hora dice
el día que vendrá.

Expositions

Strange the one who shows
himself to himself, the
mirrors lie, you know, and the wood
from the coffin in sight
fixes nothing.
Eternity's eye withered
turns the moon beautiful
and the blood here below
looks like silver. Silver
is the invincible dream, the desire
bullets can't kill.
Tomorrow is another day says
the day gone past.
I'm not on time says
the day to come.

Caramba

la muerte que adolece de
tantos defectos/véase
la gloria de este día/los pajaros
cantando en otra cosa/la
decisión de los perros que viven
su exterioridad que no perdona/
ningún astro que se oponga en la tarde
sin paradero conocido/
el puente de uno a lo que fue
caminado por cifras inconexas/
el ser que quiere ser con lámparas
que le digan dónde encontrar los lirios/
los que le perfumaron el estar
en agujeros negros/

A Rodolfo Alonso

Caramba

death suffering from
so many defects/see
the glory of this day/the birds
singing standoffish/the
decision of the dogs that live
their unforgiving outwardness/
no astral opposed in the evening
with whereabouts unknown/
the bridge from one to what was
walked by disjointed ciphers/
the being who strives to be with lamps
that tell it where to find the irises/
those that perfumed the passing
in black holes/

To Rodolfo Alonso

Gran lástima sería

La neblina de la palabra en
la neblina del mundo.
La piedra ahí,
el corazón de la piedra ahí,
en la cárcel de donde no saldrá.
La voz de la pantera
no deja dormir, salta
para agarrar la carne del sueño.
¿La escalerita al futuro tiene
los escalones rotos?
¿El tiempo la trepará llevándome?
¿No a mí, sino al sabor
del fracaso de la aventura donde
nace otra aventura?

A Great Shame It Would Be

The haze of the word in
the haze of the world.
The stone there,
the heart of the stone there,
in the prison it will never leave.
The panther's voice
keeps everyone up, jumps
to snare dream's flesh.
Does the tiny staircase to the future have
broken steps?
Will time climb it carrying me?
Not me, but the savor
of the adventure's failure where
another adventure is born?

Cortesías

Las memorias de la memoria
se van a cruel formalidad. ¿Qué mares/
nieblas/naufragios/
atravesó para llegar?/¿No recuerda
cómo singló la duda
que la esperanza en su nave puso?/
¿la noche sin dormir de no murió?/
¿la de murió?/¿el
horizonte negado?/¿la
meditación que no medita y crece
como una flor silvestre?/¿y el deseo
que no sabe desear?/¿o roto
por tiempo que pasó gastado por
cada noche/cada día/cada noche?
¿Dónde callás, memoria?/dónde
te acordás de vos misma/
acechando al verdugo para
matarlo como él te mató?

Courtesies

The memories of memory
go to cruel formality. What seas/
mists/shipwrecks/
did it cross to get here?/Doesn't it remember
how it sailed the doubt
hope placed in its ship?/
the night sleepless from didn't die/
the one from did die?/the
denied horizon?/the
meditation not meditating and growing
like a wildflower?/and the desire
not knowing how to desire?/or broken
by time passed worn out by
every night/every day/every night?
Where do you fall silent, memory?/where
do you recall yourself/
waylaying the executioner to
kill him like he killed you?

El otro

Un caballo púrpura al fondo
de una palabra ciega y
la pregunta de siempre:
¿quién escribió eso? Yo no.
Yo voy a la tienda a comprar pan
y tomo ocho medicamentos por día
para que la muerte me espere más tarde.
El caballo se mueve y la palabra
se sube al mes de abril y canta amor
a una mujer, su peso
de ave en la rama. Yo
no escribí eso, ¿de dónde, cuándo, cómo?
Yo me afeito todos los días
frente a un espejo acostumbrado.
Hoy preguntó por el caballo púrpura.
¿Y a mí me lo pregunta?
¿A mí?

A Luis García Montero

The Other

A purple horse in the depths
of a blind word and
the same old question:
who wrote that? Not me.
I go to the store to buy bread
and take eight medications a day
so death can wait a while longer.
The horse moves and the word
mounts the month of April and sings love
to a woman, her weight
a bird on a branch. I
didn't write that, where, when, how?
I shave everyday
in front of a usual mirror.
Today it asked about the purple horse.
It's asking me?
Me?

To Luis García Montero

Paulina

Tus ojos/soñabas con
abrazos de fuego. Moriste
por carta y por
las lágrimas que
guardabas en tu corazón
y les prohibías salir a la calle.
Mujer de vos como una casa
con el vaivén del piano.
Las manos que cosían
recuerdos viejos/
sílabas íntimas/desgracias.
Dejaste un hijo irreal con penas
que apuestan contra sí mismas.
O fierros maltratados
que no tocás.

Paulina

Your eyes/you dreamt of
fiery embraces. You died
by letter and by
the tears
you kept in your heart
and wouldn't let out on the street.
Woman of you like a house
with the piano's sway.
The hands sewing
old memories/
intimate syllables/disgraces.
You left an unreal son with sorrows
that bet against themselves.
Oh mistreated irons
you do not touch.

Hechos

Amor, tu cara negra
cae en la parte grosera del
corazón y hace un agujero.
Tu cara blanca
es el querer contra el no
querer/es la piedra
que da luz al principio.
Bosques de la juventud
donde perdimos todo y
ganamos todo con la piel jugada.
¿Quién te conoce, amor,
si no nos conocés?
¿Si tu péndulo tiene
el vaivén de dos caras?

Facts

Love, your black face
falls in the rough share of the
heart and digs a hole.
Your white face
is affection against no
affection/it's the stone
that sheds light on the principle.
Forests of youth
where we lost everything and
won everything with our skins at risk.
Who knows you, love,
if you don't know us?
If your pendulum bears
the swaying of two faces?

Doble

El doble sol, el de adentro y el
de afuera, queman. Flota
un hilito perdido entre los dos.
En las noches de primavera suaves
la luna vegetal vigila.
¿Y eso qué
tiene que ver con la mano que lleva
rosas en su rincón? ¿Para el tiempo
en ese gesto dulce? ¿Se detiene
y no mueren las rosas
en el rincón de la mano? ¿Qué piensa
en las inmensidades del cristal
desconocidas entre vos y yo?
¿Amor que nos queremos sin saber?
¿Esa ignorancia con
palabras en el medio?

Double

The double sun, the one inside and the one
outside, burn. A tiny lost thread
floats between the two.
In the soft spring nights
the vegetal moon keeps watch.
And what does that
have to do with the hand holding
roses in its corner? Does time stop
in that sweet gesture? Does it linger
and the roses don't die
in the hand's corner? What's it thinking
in the glass immensities
unknown between you and me?
Love we love unknowing?
That ignorance with
words in the way?

No ser sabe

Ese cantar casi río que
cunde cuando
la ventana se asoma a vos
con tardes altas en la mano y
sabe de ti más que yo/esa
espiral que va
de vos en vos y entiende
el silabario de la pérdida
en el revés del ser/ese asiento
donde nadie se sienta y no
contesta otra pregunta que
la que no se puede hacer/oh, bella
siempre nueva
entre animales del dolor/
entreabrís las palabras
para ver qué callaron.

A Mara

Not Being Knows

That well-nigh river song
swelling when
the window peeps out from you
with high evenings in its hand and
knows more about you than I/that
spiral spans
from you to you and understands
the syllabary of the loss
in the underside of being/that seat
where no one's sitting and doesn't
answer any other question than
the one that can't be asked/oh, fair one
always new
among ache's animals/
you open words halfway
to see what they silenced.

To Mara

Alambres

En la farándula del viento
colgué las ropas de mi amor. Qué vuelo
tuvo entonces el tiempo que
nos pasamos el uno al otro/tan
difícil de agarrar completo.
Estamos en
lo que nos faltamos. Allí
nos vemos el uno al otro
en una calle donde
la luz cae al revés.

A Mara

Wires

On the showbiz of the wind
I hung my love's clothes. What flight
the time we passed
each other had then/so
hard to completely grasp.
We are in
what we miss. There
we see each other
on a street where
the light falls inside out.

To Mara

Dice

¿Quién/qué?/Eso que oigo
y no entiendo
lo digo yo. Se presenta
el ser que no es
y los pájaros llaman al crepúsculo.
Ojalá me dieran un lugar
en su nido para ser útil/no
esta deriva de la
lengua que me heriste en la cuna.
No te conozco todavía.
Te cavo
para saber quién soy.

Says

Who/what?/What I hear
and don't understand
is what I'm saying. The being
that isn't appears
and the birds call out to twilight.
I could only hope they give me a spot
in their nest to be useful/not
this drifting of my
tongue you wounded in the cradle.
I still don't know you.
I hollow you
to know who I am.

A veces

Sin saludo ni aviso
la ciudad se goza a solas
en un domingo tierno.
¿Y quién es uno entonces?
La memoria se calla
y la hermosura de las calles
prohíbe el paso del dolor.
Todo es afuera, dice.
Lo que te toca es una calle
ávida de puertos donde no
partirás de esta calle nunca.

At Times

With no welcome or warning
the city enjoys itself alone
on a tender Sunday.
So who is one then?
Memory falls silent
and the beauty of the streets
forbids ache's passing.
Everything's outside, it says.
What you're left with is a street
greedy for ports where you won't
part from this street ever.

Sirenas

En la intemperie del poema cantan
sirenas y no hay que
hacerles caso. La palabra navega. ¿Y esa mano
qué quiere decir? ¿Quién la puso
aquí mismo en escándalos de
lo bien amado/el odio
a lo que bien se ama? Las criaturas
seguras del abismo parlan,
recuperan la pérdida
para perderla otra vez. Ahora
el color rojo es piedra que
golpea palabras.

Sirens

In the poem's inclemency sing
sirens and you need not
take any notice of them. The word sails. And that
    hand
what does it mean? Who put it
right here in scandals of
the beloved/the hate
of what's beloved? The creatures
certain of the abyss chatter,
regain the loss
to lose it once more. Now
the color red is stone
striking words.

Tal vez

La gaviota acaricia lo
que no sabe volar. Así los pobres
con decisión del alma cuelan
estrellas en su cuarto, brillan más
que las constelaciones y la noche
se aposenta en su soñar bajito.
¡Animales del deseo que
no dejan dormir y se vuelven
compañeros de vida!
¡Alzan las furias de la mano
vacía en cruz de piedra! Unir
lo que se sabe a lo ignorado, los
pedazos que vendrán y que
calientan en el miedo, áspero
de clavos fríos en
los parientes más queridos del alma.

Perhaps

The seagull caresses what
doesn't know how to fly. Like so the poor
with soul decision strain
stars in their rooms, they shine brighter
than the constellations and the night
dwells in its dreaming so low.
Animals of desire
keep everyone up and become
comrades in life!
Raise empty hand's furies
in a stone cross! To unite
what's known with the unknown, the
pieces to come and to
warm in the fear, rough
with cold nails in
the soul's dearest kinfolk.

Cifras

Las gotas en la mesa
no son lágrimas. El solazo
las evapora al otro lado
de la tela que tejemos con
alguna desesperación. ¿Qué pasa
en estas tierras sin oír? El mar
en los dedos parece
un mineral que no se queda, una
hermana que fallece en
la mitad del corazón o la mañana
sin huellas que se va
a lo que enciende el sufrimiento.
Hay que estar atento a
las señales que fabrican
su propia sombra. Crecen
los pájaros detrás. Oír,
oír el río que pasa
cada alma que pasa
encima de la sopa de
letras de hueso.

Ciphers

The drops on the table
aren't tears. The scorching sun
evaporates them on the other side
of the cloth we weave
somewhat desperately. What's
happening in these lands unheard? The sea
in the fingers seems like
a mineral unremaining, a
sister who dies in
the heart's middle or the traceless
morning that shifts
to what suffering kindles.
You've got to be alert to
the signs that make up
their own shadow. The birds
grow behind them. To hear,
to hear the river flow
each soul that flows
over the soup
of bone letters.

La sed

En esos prados donde
dejóse y olvidóse hoy crecen
inviernos y el vacío. El vio
ciervos de aire cruzando
su sed de amor.
Esos flujos de sombra que arden
tan lejos, don San Juan, interrogaban
lo que no es porque no es.
Es la única forma de vivir,
padre dulce, insaciable.
El agua que no has de beber
moja la mano que te escribe.

The Thirst

In those meadows where
he gave in and forgot today grow
winters and the void. He saw
wind's deer crossing
his thirst for love.
Those shadow flows burning
so far off, don Saint John, questioned
what isn't because it isn't.
It's the only way to live,
sweet, insatiable father.
The water you don't drink
dampens the hand that writes you.

Estaba

Cuando todos los miembros del cuerpo
son vos, puerta nocturna
que abre ciega a la dicha,
el tamaño del tiempo es una luna
que alumbra lo que fuimos.
El pensamiento, un dedo libre
que hojea páginas pasadas.
Los años no obedecen, suena
un violín mudo. La piel quema
lo que hubo, tan lejos.
Te picotean los gorriones
que comieron mi pan.

A Mara

Was

When all the limbs of the body
are you, nocturnal door
opening blind to happiness,
the size of time is a moon
lightening what we were.
Thought, a free finger
leafing through past pages.
The years don't obey, a mute
violin sounds. The skin burns
what was, so far-off.
You're pecked by the sparrows
that ate my bread.

To Mara

Árboles

Quien se inclina a
recoger un papel del suelo ve
que los árboles hablan. Esto
no va a ninguna parte. Preguntar
qué dijeron antes
de que los derribaran no
va a ninguna parte. Los árboles
tocan la mañana para que sea feliz y eso
es un destino y no
va a ninguna parte. Una sierra
les saca pájaros del día,
la tarde no se acuesta cantada.
Mi mesa es un silencio
que no se puede abrir.

Trees

Whoever bends down to
pick a piece of paper off the floor sees
that the trees speak. This
is going nowhere. To ask
what they said before
they were fallen is
going nowhere. The trees
touch the morning so it's happy and that's
a destiny and it's
going nowhere. A saw
clears away day's birds,
the evening doesn't lie down sung.
My table is a silence
that can't be opened.

La espiral

En cada punto, un rostro
de mí que no es de mí. Que callen
las ventanas, el mundo.
¿Qué hago aquí al pie de una palabra
que no se deja decir?
Inútil perseguirla, ella sabe
que su única casa es ella misma.
Ya nunca entenderé cómo cantan los grillos
que cincelan la noche.
En ese animalito cabe
la lejanía del estar. La noche
que me cubre la mano
otoña en nieblas idas
y los motivos lentos
dan frío al corazón.

The Spiral

At each point, a face
of mine that isn't mine. Let
the windows, the world fall silent.
What am I doing here at the foot of a word
that refuses to be said?
It's useless to shadow it, it knows
its only house is itself.
Now I'll never understand how the crickets
sing chiseling the night.
In that tiny animal fits
the distance of passing. The night
covering my hand
autumns in gone mists
and the slow motives
cool the heart.

Semillas

En la aventura de la tarde
creció una voz extraña. ¿Era
el negro vértigo de ser? Amor,
¿sos vértigo de ser? ¿Por qué
das luz como el pan que
leo en tus labios? Clavo
mis dientes en el instinto de
los patios de la infancia con
plantas que bebían
el agua de mi madre.
No conozco quién soy, regreso
de mí a mí, fugado
de la aglomeración de los trabajos.
Ahora están quietos los diamantes
que ponés en la mesa
como señal de vos.

Seeds

In evening's adventure
grew a strange voice. Was it
the black vertigo of being? Love,
are you vertigo of being? Why
do you shed light like the bread
I read on your lips? I sink
my teeth into the instinct of
infancy's courtyards with
plants that drank
my mother's water.
I don't know who I am, I return
from me to me, on the run
from the agglomeration of work.
Now they're still, the diamonds
you place on the table
as a sign of you.

Mendigos

La moneda cae
con su país sin alma.
Nadie vive en el himno que
cantan los escolares y
la gloria que pasó, ya lejos.
Inmóvil,
el Poder abre abismos en
el sonido de cada uno, único.
¿Quién reconoce su mitad
con delicias soñadas?
Soñar es un trabajo que
adentro no separa la
tierra del cielo. El cuerpo mira
las manos que podrían
tocar otoños que vendrán,
claros, la dicha me
calla escondida.

Beggars

The coin falls
with its soulless country.
No one lives in the anthem
sung by school children and
the glory passed, now far-off.
Unmoving,
the Power opens abysses in
the sound of each one, only.
Who knows their half
with dreamt-of delights?
To dream is work that
inside doesn't separate the
earth from the sky. The body looks
at the hands that might
touch autumns to come,
clear, happiness
silences me hidden.

Así, así

la piel revienta/el alma
o lo que así se llama/
no se quiere sentar/¿qué ciencia
le dará paz?/no tiene
otros parientes que el absurdo
de reír victorias que no son/
resplandece la luna en
noches que burlan su destino y
¿quién podría nombrar al pasado
de este presente seco?/el gran fondo
de las fosas que el poema recuerda
no tiene huesos sino
la inocencia de noches caminadas
por el miedo a no ser/

A María Negroni

So, So

the skin bursts/the soul
or whatever's called so/
doesn't want to sit down/what science
might give it peace?/it has no
other kin than the nonsense
of laughing victories that aren't/
the moon shines in
nights that outsmart their destiny and
who could name the past
of this dry present?/the great depth
of the graves the poem remembers
doesn't have bones but rather
the innocence of nights walked
by the fear of not being/

To María Negroni

Descubrimientos

Derrota/leo tu libro/
maestra íntima/ya libre
de vos/¿qué ángel caído
hay en tu espalda?/vos/
tan siempre/vi tu cara
un día que volabas
de vos a mí/endemientras
el deseo levantaba su furia
en las desgracias del amor.
El cerca lejos de
tu despego sin alma
resplandece en servicios
de tu voz/y la
conciencia de lo amado.
Me recrearas en tu flujo
donde llorás más que yo.

Discoveries

Defeat/I read your book/
intimate mistress/now free
of you/what fallen angel
is there on your back?/you/
so always/I saw your face
one day you were flying
from you to me/in the meantime
the desire raised its fury
in love's disgraces.
The nearness far from
your soulless detachment
shines at the services
of your voice/and the
consciousness of the loved.
Perhaps you recreated me in your flow
where you cry more than I.

Neblinas

Las del dolor y sus noches salvajes
secan la forma, el color de
Venus en la noche arriba. El olor
a miseria o costumbre
pasa debajo de la cama que
no duerme y abre
los pensamientos. Qué
sucede en las aguas donde
lavamos nuestros rostros.
Pregunten a
las carcajadas de la sombra.

Hazes

Those of ache and its savage nights
dry out the shape, the color of
Venus in the night above. The scent
of wretchedness or habit
slips beneath the bed not
sleeping and opens
the thoughts. What
happens in the waters where
we wash our faces?
Ask
the shadow's laughter.

Translator's Note

The translation of Hildegard of Bingen comes from *The Personal Correspondence of Hildegard of Bingen*. Joseph L. Baird, ed. Baird and Radd K. Ehrman, trans. Oxford: Oxford UP, 2006.

All other translations are the sole responsibility of the translators.

www.ingramcontent.com/pod-product-compliance
Lightning Source LLC
Chambersburg PA
CBHW022000100426
42738CB00042B/995